Prayers

THAT OPEN THE

PORTALS
OF HEAVEN

Prayers
THAT OPEN THE
PORTALS
OF HEAVEN

SONYA HURST

Get
WR TE
PUBLISHING

PRAYERS THAT OPEN THE PORTALS OF HEAVEN

Copyright © 2016 by Sonya Hurst

All scripture quotations, unless otherwise indicated, were taken from the King James Version and Strong's Concordance in The Blue Letter Bible.

ISBN 978-1-945456-35-0

Printed in the United States of America.

Cover Design: KDV Design & Associates

Editors: Apostle Jonathan Hurst, Barbara Merriwether & John Merriwether Jr.

Dedication

I would like to give honor to my Heavenly Father, the one and only true and living God. You have taken me to another dimension in life and for that I am grateful. Thank you for calling me forth to intercede for Your people. Out of my obedience to Your call, You have birthed multiple new facets in my life. I proclaim Jesus is my savior and I thank God for His Holy Spirit who is my guide.

To my loving husband, Jonathan, thank you for sharing this life with me. I am grateful to God for your love and support. God has truly blessed me with a man of God after His heart. I am looking forward to the dynamic ministry that God has for the two of us.

To my children, Deborah, Gabrielle and two in heaven, I am grateful that God has blessed us with protecting, loving and guiding you. You all have greatness in you. We love you to life.

To my parents, I am grateful for your faith and love for God. You both have trained your children to love and fear God. Your strength and character have overflowed to us. I love and thank you.

To my 95-year-old grandmother, I thank you for showing your entire family how to fear, love and live a life sold out to God. Your legacy will continue with the foundation that you have laid. May God grant your prayer to live to see 100 years. I love you.

To my siblings, you all have greatness in you. I love you.

To my Pastor Joel Osteen, thank you for sharing your many testimonies of being called by God to Pastor without formal training. You have shown many that God can take you further and faster than anything or anyone else can. I have enjoyed the story of how you put your feet in the late Pastor

John Osteen shoes in the beginning of your Pastoring. I also enjoy watching God use you to pour hope into so many people who need hope. You have encouraged, inspired and pushed me to be better with encouraging words that I can do whatever God said I can do. I have been equipped. You have sewn several books into my life, written many encouraging letters, notes, and messages. I am honored to serve on the prayer partner team under your leadership at Lakewood Church. I thank you and love you and your family.

To my mentors and supernatural connection to Apostles Christopher and Pamela Hardy, you have changed my life. What a tremendous blessing to meet such loving leaders in the Kingdom of God. Apostle Christopher was able to train me as a minister and pull greatness out of me. Thank you

To my prayer partner, Della Parks, thank you for standing on the wall with me in prayer. What an amazing journey we have had through our prayer partnership.

To my Lakewood Church prayer partner team, I love you all and I am so grateful to serve with you. May God continue to show us multiple levels in Him as we continue on this journey together. Thank you for your prayers and support.

Acknowledgements

I would like to thank all those who financially supported this project. I love you. May God bless you for your faithfulness and heart of love.

Jimmy & Shirley Davis
Edna Morrow
Della Parks
Lisa Jones
Oscar Anderson
Natasha McCrae

CONTENTS

PART I: PRAYERS FOR FAMILY

PART II: PRAYERS FOR A STRENGTHENED VESSEL

PART III: PRAYERS FOR POWER

PART IV: SPIRITUAL WARFARE PRAYERS

PART V: PRAYERS FOR THE WORLD

PART VI: PRAYERS FOR ECONOMIC GROWTH & DEVELOPMENT

Foreword

God has begun a new divine season of raising up prayer warriors in the earth realm. These new prayer generals are leading the charge in advancing the Kingdom of God! These Kingdom prayer generals are rising up and taking their place on the front lines of prayer and intercession. Here, we have a prayer general by the name of Apostle Sonya Hurst! She and her husband are two prayer generals who I have come to adore and respect highly in the Kingdom of God!

Throughout our lives, we have been taught that prayer consists of daily rudiments of religion, but not so! Prayer in its simplest form is communicating with our Supreme King, Yahweh! To understand prayer, it's necessary to understand the mind and purpose of the Creator, God Himself. What we have to know and realize is that prayer is not an option. Prayer is a necessity! I believe this book, Prayers that Open The Portals of Heaven, is a must read for those that find themselves on the front lines of prayer and for those that just want to understand that prayer can open portals over any situation!

God does answer prayer, but He does not answer all of them immediately! When Daniel prayed for twenty-one days and received no answer, something was still happening. His days of prayer opened a portal for the access of God's sovereign will to begin to work through that portal.

This beautifully crafted prayer book penned by Apostle Sonya, depicts the portals that will form once you start praying for everything mentioned in this book. As you and your prayer teams pray for singles, let that portal form. As you pray for purpose and alignment let the portals form. As you pray against a spirit of suicide, let the portals form! Through those portals, like in Daniel's day, God will respond with angels sent from His Presence to overthrow the Prince of Darkness and withstand his demons in the earth! That's the power of prayer portals and that is what you will read in this book. You will also learn the strategies of prayer.

These are exciting times and this book is very exciting to me. God desires to partner with you as you read and pray with Him regarding these passages. Partner with Him in the great purpose of reclaiming and redeeming the world through prayer. The Scripture continues to say; "If my people, who are called by my name, will humble themselves and pray and seek my face and turn from their wicked ways, then will I hear from heaven and will forgive their sin and will heal their land" (II Chronicles 7:14).

Prayer is an invitation for God to intervene in our affairs, such as our marriages, families, careers, homes, communities, ministries and nations of the earth. Prayer is also our agreement with His sovereign will at our request for The King to work His ways and His works in the world. Enjoy this much needed book! It is necessary for the Kingdom of God to advance in the earth. Prayers that Open the Portals of Heaven! Blessings & Answers Manifest, B.A.M!

Apostle Christopher J. Hardy
International Covenant Life Network
Kingdom Ambassadors Center
Kingdom Ambassadors Ministerial Training
Eagles International Business Institute

INTRODUCTION
Prayer - Our Tool to Activate Heaven on Earth
(A Powerful Weapon used by Kingdom Ambassadors of Heaven on Earth)

———————— ~ ————————

This is a practical book that is a war cry to Heaven to open up the portals to not only hear our prayers but to answer them. Prayer invites God to operate in the lives of His believers. Therefore, prayer brings Heaven to earth. Jesus taught the disciples to pray and said, "Thy kingdom come. Thy will be done in earth, as it is in heaven" (Matthew 6:10). In the book of Daniel, the portal of Heaven was open for Daniel after twenty-one days of fasting and prayer. The book of Daniel states, "Then said he unto me, Fear not, Daniel: for from the first day that thou didst set thine heart to understand, and to chasten thyself before thy God, thy words were heard, **AND I AM COME FOR THY WORDS**" (Daniel 10:12).

Prayer is simply communication with God. Prayer is also a strategic weapon of the mind and tongue to release fire from Heaven to defeat the enemy and receive answers to prayers. The bible says there is power in what you say. Proverbs says, "Death and life are in the power of the tongue: and they that love it shall eat the fruit thereof" (Proverbs 18:21). That means when you open your mouth and speak whether it is in prayer or speaking casually, you have the power to release life and death. Therefore, when you pray, open your mouth and allow that powerful weapon to release life into yours. No time for silent prayers, since you have a more powerful weapon when you speak it out loud.

In the following pages, there are strategic prayers to pray daily for specific situations. There will be an area where you can journal the words God is speaking to you. There is also a space for the date the prayer request(s) was made and answered. Before each prayer in your natural language; pray in your spiritual language. Pray in the Spirit because the Word of God says, "Likewise the Spirit also helpeth our infirmities: for **we know not what we should pray for as we ought: but the Spirit itself maketh intercession for us with groanings which cannot be uttered**" (Romans 8:26). Praying in tongues gives a supernatural understanding of the mysteries of God, revelatory knowledge, truth, wisdom, guidance, and power (1 Corinthians 14:2, 1 Corinthians 2:10, John 16:13, Acts 1:8, Ephesians 6:18). Therefore, if you have not received your gift of speaking in tongues, you can receive it today. First, you must accept Jesus Christ as your Lord and Savior. Jesus said, "I am the way, the truth, and the life: no man cometh unto the Father, but by me" (John 14:6). So, "if thou shalt confess with thy mouth the Lord Jesus, and shalt believe in thine heart that God hath raised him from the dead, thou shalt be saved" (Romans 10:9). Next, you're ready for the fire baptism. Fire baptism is the Holy Spirit. Ask God to fill you with His Holy Spirit. Jesus answered, "Verily, verily, I say unto thee, except a man be born of water and of the Spirit, he cannot enter into the kingdom of God" (John 3:5). Jesus expounds, "For John truly baptized with water; but ye shall be baptized with the

Holy Ghost not many days hence. But ye shall receive power, after that the Holy Ghost is come upon you: and ye shall be witnesses unto me both in Jerusalem, and in all Judaea, and in Samaria, and unto the uttermost part of the earth" (Acts 1:5, 8). Then, Ask God to give you the gift of tongues. The book of John says, "And whatsoever ye shall ask in my name, that will I do, that the Father may be glorified in the Son. If ye shall ask any thing in my name, I will do it" (John 14:13-14). Finally, open your mouth and pray in your natural language out loud while asking God to pour out His Spirit on you and give you the gift of speaking in tongues. Release your inabilities unto God. Raise your hands to the Father in an attitude of submission and surrender to God. Receive it. Receive it. Receive it. Power! Why do you need this you may ask? We just read what Jesus said, "You shall receive **POWER**" (Acts1:8). When you pray in tongues you are speaking directly to the Father. Paul explains praying in tongues, "For he that speaketh in an unknown tongue speaketh not unto men, but unto God: for no man understandeth him; howbeit in the spirit he speaketh mysteries" (1 Corinthians 14:2). Now that you have received understanding and power, **LET'S GO TO WAR!**

PART I: PRAYERS FOR FAMILY

PRAYER FOR MARRIAGE COVENANTS

Dear Heavenly Father, thank You for the understanding that marriage is the highest covenant relationship that You formed in the process of creation. Father, You said it is not good for man to be alone, so You created woman from man's rib (Genesis 2:22-23). Your Word says, "Therefore shall a man leave his father and his mother, and shall cleave unto his wife: and they shall be one flesh" (Genesis 2:24). Therefore, we are no longer two but one, and "what therefore God hath joined together, let not man put asunder" (Mathew 19:6). Because we are one, we are in one accord, speaking the same language and always in unity and therefore, nothing is withheld from us according to Your Word God (Genesis 11:6). We have the anointing and power of God because we are in unity. The anointing oil and fragrance of God saturates our union. (Psalm 133:1-3). We are examples and ensamples to others because we are saved, filled with the Spirit of God and walk in the Spirit daily (1 Peter 5:3). We commit to agreeing quickly and live in peace with one another as not to allow Satan any room in our union (Mathew 5:25, Romans 12:18). Your Word says, "Two are better than one because we get a good reward for our labor" (Ecclesiastes 4:9). Therefore, we seek to stay together. The enemy will not infiltrate our marriage with anything or anyone. Therefore, "what God has put together, no man" will ever be able to destroy (Mathew 19:6, Mark 10:9). Christ is in the center of our marriage which makes us a threefold bond. Therefore, we are two that will withstand anything because Your Word declares, "two shall withstand him; and a threefold cord is not quickly broken" (Ecclesiastes 4:12). We are able to hold each other up in trying times and encourage one another (Ecclesiastes 4:10). Divorce is not an option because it is the government of this world and we live by the Word of God. Marriage was never designed by man, but God, and was designed to be a lifetime commitment while on earth. Jesus said, "Moses because of the hardness of your hearts, suffered you to put away your wives: but from the beginning it was not so" (Mathew 19:8). Therefore, divorce will not be so in our marriage. We are not held by the standards of this world but by the standards of God. We, therefore, will not take part in adultery because of the world's standards (Mathew 19:9). We enjoy each other emotionally, intellectually, spiritually and physically. We now have the right to enjoy each other sexually because we are in a covenant marriage. We have now been given the command to "be fruitful and multiply" (Genesis 1:28). Therefore, my "breast shall satisfy" my "husband always" (Proverb 5:19). We will never have to look for spoil because we satisfy each other's needs (Proverb 5:20, Proverbs 31:11). We are enjoying one another and we are ravished with each other's love all the days of our lives (Proverbs 5:19). I decree it to be so, by the power given to me, by the infallible Holy Word of God, in Jesus name, Amen.

My ears are open to hear your voice. Speak Lord!

_____

_____

Date Prayer Request Released   Date Prayer Answered

_____   _____

PRAYER FOR THE WOMB
(HEALTHY REPRODUCTION)

Heavenly Father, I decree that at Your Word, You gave the command to be fruitful and multiply to husband and wife (Genesis 1:28). Therefore, I decree that my womb is fruitful and we will multiply according to the Word of God. My womb is healthy and free from all abnormalities. I decree Your Word, "Lo, children are an heritage of the Lord: and the fruit of the womb is his reward" (Psalm 127:3). Father, You created my womb to reproduce. Therefore, whatever is blocking or hindering my reproductive organ to reproduce, I call it out now. My womb is functioning as it was designed to function. My fallopian tubes are open and free to allow the fertilized egg to travel to the healthy lining of my womb. Every child that You allow in my womb is healthy and will be birthed at the appointed time and will not move out of the timing of God. Father, Jacob prayed for his wife Rebekah to conceive and You formed two nations from that womb (Genesis 25:23-24). So I declare that my husband is praying and anointing my womb to prepare me to deliver children that will be birthed for the nations. You said to Jeremiah, "Before I formed thee in the belly I knew thee; and before thou camest forth out of the womb I sanctified thee, and I ordained thee a prophet unto the nations" (Jeremiah 1:5). So You Lord have a purpose and a plan for every seed that is placed in my womb and birthed at the appointed time. I declare, "For all the promises of God in him are yea, and in

5

him Amen..." (2 Corinthians 1:20). I have the same faith as Abraham, that You will birth many destined, blessed, anointed and appointed children from my womb (Romans 4:19-21). My trust is in You Lord for You are not a man that You would lie nor have to repent (Numbers 23:19). Therefore, I trust Your Word, Lord. I am, "fully assured that what God had promised, He was able also to perform" (Romans 4:19-21). Lord keep me around anointed people of God that make my children leap in my womb and when birthed out of my womb. I have people that speak, "Blessed are you among women, and blessed is the fruit of your womb" (Luke 1:41-45). Father God, remember me and open my womb as You did for Rachel when you gave heed to her and opened her womb" (Genesis 30:22-23). Because Lord You are not a respecter of persons I believe that just as You did for Hannah, Rachel and many women You will do the same for me (1 Samuel 1:11-20, Acts 10:34, Romans 2:11). I decree it to be so, by the power given to me, by the infallible Holy Word of God, in Jesus name, Amen.

My ears are open to hear your voice. Speak Lord!

_____

_____

Date Prayer Request Released   Date Prayer Answered

_____   _____

6

PRAYER FOR CHILDREN

Heavenly Father, because children are a heritage and a reward from the Lord, my children are blessed (Psalm 127:3). My children are mighty in the land (Psalm 112:2). My children are chosen for such a time as this. My children have a heritage in the Kingdom of God because they are saved and filled with the Holy Spirit. Hence, my children know and follow the voice of the Father (John 10:4). Therefore, I decree and declare Your Word over my children that, "a stranger they will not follow, but will flee from him: for they know not the voice of strangers" (John 10:5). I declare that peer pressure is no pressure at all. My children are leaders and set the mark. Therefore, other children want to follow their example of a Godly lifestyle. My children are functioning and soaring as eagles (Isaiah 40:31). You have ordained my children for praise (Matthew 21:16). They flow with an apostolic anointing. Therefore, my children fear not darkness, but bring the light of God with authority, to every place that they step. My children function in excellence. They excel with high honors in school and extracurricular activities. Scholarships are chasing them down and therefore all education is covered in full. They start their adult lives debt free and continue to be debt free for the rest of their lives. My children are taught of the Lord (Isaiah 54:13). My children have the strength of the Lord. My children understand and operate as God commanded to have dominion on earth. Therefore, my children operate as

Kingdom ambassadors and citizens operating in the dominion that God created them to possess. My children are anointed for everything that God has destined them to accomplish. Because You said that children are arrows in the hands of their parents, God give us the vision to see where You would like for us to guide them (Psalm 127:4). My children have a clear future because I cancel every spiritual assignment of confusion. I decree that my children have flourishing businesses. My children own land and properties that will be used for the Kingdom of God. My children are blessed beyond measure. I pray that my children will abstain from any sexual behaviors before marriage. I pray now for God fearing mates for each of my children. I pray that my children's mates are saved and filled with the Holy Spirit. I pray that they love their parents and treat them with honor, as the Word of God has commanded. My children's mates are also eagles, destined for greatness. My children's mates will not mentally, emotionally, physically abuse or misuse my children, because they understand their gift and their purpose. My children and their mates are mentally stable because they have the mind of Christ. I decree and declare that all perverted minds of the enemy will stay away from my children. A hedge of the Blood of Jesus protects and covers them all the days of their lives. I decree that fire swells and blinds the eyes of the enemy immediately if the enemy tries to even look, to devise hurt to my children. Your Word says Lord, "A naughty person, a wicked man, walketh with a froward mouth. He winketh with his eyes, he speaketh with his feet, he teacheth with his fingers;

Frowardness is in his heart, he deviseth mischief continually; he soweth discord. Therefore shall his calamity come suddenly; suddenly shall he be broken without remedy" (Proverbs 6:12-15). Suddenly, suddenly, suddenly the Lord's judgment comes to my children's rescue that no hurt, harm or danger will ever come near their dwelling or near our children (Psalm 91:1-16). I stand and speak against premature death of my children. My children shall live and not die and declare the works of the Lord (Psalm 118:17). I declare one hundred and twenty strengthened, healthy years for my children (Genesis 6:3). My children shall never be feeble or unhealthy because they follow the decrees, commandments and have healthy lifestyles. Therefore, there is no sickness or disease in any of my children. I decree it to be so, by the power given to me, by the infallible Holy Word of God, in Jesus name, Amen.

My ears are open to hear your voice. Speak Lord!

_____

_____

Date Prayer Request Released   Date Prayer Answered

_____   _____

9

PRAYER FOR SINGLES

Dear Heavenly Father, I thank You for the preparation phase of my life for my mate. You, Lord, have prepared me for greatness and I believe that You created my mate in Your image and likeness. You also created my mate for greatness. Father God, I am clear that You made man and woman to be in a covenant marriage relationship. Therefore, I will not be confused in the preparation phase of singleness and step out of Your will to date, or be in a marriage with the same sex. Thank You Lord that You bring clarity, wisdom, knowledge and understanding of the right relationships that You Lord ordained. While I wait Lord, I pray that You will give me the strength I need to stay pure and abstain from any immoral behaviors while in preparation. Lord, Your Word says, "What things soever ye desire, when ye pray, believe that ye receive them, and ye shall have them" (Mark 11:24). Therefore, I call out my mate to come to me now. The wait is over! The preparation is over! My mate is saved, filled with the Holy Spirit, loves God, loves their family and serves God with their whole heart. Because my mate loves You Lord wholeheartedly, my mate loves me. Father Your Word says, "It is not good that the man should be alone; I will make him an help meet for him" (Genesis 2:18). Therefore, there is no confusion as to whether you made someone for me or not. If I decide to be single, it is my decision because it is clear in Your Word that You made someone for me. Because it is Your will for Your sons and daughters to have companionship, I thank You that You have already chosen and ordained the right companion for me according to Your Word. Whatever is holding up my mate is being corrected now Lord. My mate is already developed spiritually, physically, emotionally, financially and socially. I declare that You have destined me to have a mate because Your Word says that two are better than one and a threefold cord is not easily broken (Ecclesiastes 4:12). I declare that the mate that You have chosen for me only awaits the divine meeting. I thank You Lord that I will not be encumbered by unnecessary works, foolishness or any unwholesome acts, that will delay or cancel my mate wanting to be with me.

Every assignment of lust devised by the enemy is canceled now. I declare that I will not waste time on wrong relationships. Therefore, help me Lord to understand Your divine timing. I decree that I will not try to hurry the process by getting in relationships that are not in Your divine will. I declare that You Lord give me discernment for the right person to share in my life. In the process of waiting Lord, I will serve You even until the end of days. I will speak of Your goodness. I will serve You. I will praise You Lord. I will honor You Lord with my heart, my life, my walk, my being. No relationship will ever get me out of the will of God or keep me from loving You. In the divine relationship chosen for me, we serve You God together. We pray together, study Your Word and worship You Lord, together.

Father, sever the ties with old relationships that are not designed for me. I ask that You would cleanse me of all unrighteousness or impure acts of previous relationships.

Cancel every thought of those relationships that I may be free to move to higher realms in the Spirit. As we come together, the assignment of God will manifest with full force in the right direction. The anointing is upon us as we become one in marriage, as ordained by You Lord (Psalm 133:1-3). The assignments that were waiting on us to be one will manifest unhindered. The Kingdom of God is increased because we are one! I decree it to be so, by the power given to me, by the infallible Holy Word of God, in Jesus name, Amen.

My ears are open to hear your voice. Speak Lord!

_____

_____

Date Prayer Request Released   Date Prayer Answered

_____   _____

PRAYER FOR MY DWELLING PLACE

Dear Heavenly Father, I decree that my dwelling place is blessed because You are there. I decree that all inhabitants are saved and serving God. I declare, "As for me and my house, we will serve the Lord" (Joshua 24:15). Father, I dedicate my home to You. I decree that it will be a place of integrity, unity and love. My home is sanctified, anointed and filled with the Holy Spirit because it is washed daily with the Word of God from my lips (Ephesians 5:26). Father God You are welcomed here in the home that You have provided for me. I declare that my home is on a firm foundation, which is in Christ Jesus. Therefore, I declare that the foundation of my home is blessed. Every room is blessed and filled with the presence of God. The blood of the Lamb is on the doorpost of my home as a symbol to You Lord and the enemy that Your people reside in this home and all sickness, disease, destruction, plots, schemes, wicked devices, plans of the enemy pass over and leaves from my place of dwelling (Exodus 12:7, 13). Lord it is in You that I find my dwelling and "thou hast been our dwelling place in all generations" (Psalm 90:1). I declare, "There shall no evil befall thee, neither shall any plague come nigh thy dwelling" (Psalm 91:10). For You Lord, "shall give your angels charge over thee, to keep thee in all thy ways. They shall bear thee up in their hands, lest thou dash thy foot against a stone" (Psalm 91:11-12). I decree, "The angel of the Lord encampeth round about" me because I fear and reverence

Him, therefore, He delivers this house and all inhabitants (Psalm 34:7). I decree that my home is very well cared for and does not break down because the Holy Spirit gives me wisdom and discernment of the appropriate time to manage a potential issue. I decree that no pornography, inappropriate television shows, vulgar and inappropriate music, inappropriate internet adds or websites and immoral acts will ever enter into the home that You have provided for me. I decree that all inhabitants in this home have the Spirit of God living in them and feel the correction of God if even a thought of the previous mentioned acts come. I repent now Lord and ask for Your forgiveness for any previous acts committed knowingly and unknowingly by any inhabitants in this home. Any immoral acts shall cease now in Jesus name. I decree that the waring angels of God are set up at every corner of my home fighting every attempt, plot, scheme against my home and all inhabitants. I decree that the God of Abraham, Isaac and Jacob set up ambushes for the enemy that tries to come near my dwelling place. I decree that this house "shall be a house of prayer" (Isaiah 56:7). I declare that this house shall also be a place of love. All friends and family that visits finds the love of God and is welcomed. I decree it to be so, by the power given to me, by the infallible Holy Word of God, in Jesus name, Amen.

My ears are open to hear your voice. Speak Lord!

_____

_____

Date Prayer Request Released   Date Prayer Answered

_____   _____

PRAYER TO BREAK GENERATIONAL CURSES

Heavenly Father, I decree because I love You and follow Your commandments, that You show Your mercy to me and every generation connected to me (Exodus 20:6). I lay before You every sin of any one in my blood line that has committed anything that You hate such as: lust, idolatry, adultery, incest, homosexuality, murder, theft, gossip, lying tongue, pride, a heart that devises wicked imaginings, feet swift in running to mischief, bearing false witness, and sowing discord among brethren (Proverbs 6:16-19). I decree that Jesus paid the price for every sin of commission and omission for me and every generation before and after me. Father God I repent for all sins of my forefathers. I ask for forgiveness of all generations before and after me. I decree and declare that the blood line of every family name connected to me (call out the surnames connected to you) is free from any generational sin and curse because we receive the knowledge of Jesus Christ, repent from all sin and accept Christ as our personal savior. Therefore, we are free from any curse because Jesus Christ makes us free (Galatians 3:13). I shout aloud by the authority of Jesus, "If the son therefore shall make you free, YE SHALL BE FREE INDEED" (John 8:36)! I thank you Abba Father that You sent Jesus Christ to release my family from any sin in any generation connected to me. Lord I cry out for my family! I cry out for the repentance of the heart of my family from desires of the flesh, anger, bitterness, lying, stealing, murder and not loving our neighbor!

Your Word says that our body is the temple of the Holy Spirit. I know that the Holy Spirit will not dwell in sin, so I decree and declare that a swift understanding comes to my family that no one else will be affected by our wicked ways. Sin causes death and therefore, I will make a conscious effort not to sin and to live Holy as the Lord God is Holy. I decree that my family members and I will follow the commandments of God because we hide the Word in our hearts (Psalm 119:11). I break any generational curse trying to attach itself to my bloodline at the very root of its existence and burn it beyond recognition. Every generation connected to me has found their dwelling place in You Lord (Psalm 90:1). I confess that my family is the generation that seeks the Lord (Psalm 24:6). Father, I declare that the Word of God, the worship, praise, reverence and honor of the only living Holy God, will be transferred from my generation to the last generation before Christ comes (Psalm 78:4-11). We will never hide from You or Your word **JEHOVAH QADASH (KA-DASH)** the Lord that sanctifies and makes holy (Psalm 78:4-11, Leviticus 20:8, Ezekiel 37:28, Strong# 6942). I decree it to be so, by the power given to me, by the infallible Holy Word of God, in Jesus name, Amen.

My ears are open to hear your voice. Speak Lord!

_____

_____

Date Prayer Request Released   Date Prayer Answered

_____   _____

PART II: PRAYERS FOR A
STRENGTHENED VESSEL

PRAYER FOR HEALING

Abba Father, I cry out to You for healing in my body and the body of Christ. You Lord sent Your Word to heal all of the diseases and infirmities that was introduced by sin in the world. You said it is Your desire that we be "healthy and prosper even as our soul prospers" (3 John 1:2). Therefore, it is not Your desire that Your people perish. So I command my body and Your son's and daughter's bodies to come in perfect alignment with Your Word. We shall not be weak, feeble, in pain, sickly or diseased because we have the power of God, the creator in our bodies. I take authority over my body and the body of Christ to be healed. I declare, **BREAKTHROUGH HEALING NOW** Lord! I decree and declare my muscles, tendons, organs and every cell in my body is healthy. I speak the light of God the creator of my body to **DISSIPATE, DISINTEGRATE, DEMOLISH, ERADICATE, UPROOT, ANNIHILATE, OBLIB-ERATE** and **DISMANTLE anything** that is not of You God and illegally residing in my body. God You have given me power to pray Your will on earth as it is in Heaven (Mathew 6:10). Therefore, I say that cancer, diabetes, high blood pressure, tumors, deformities, headaches, back aches, reproductive disorders, blood disorders, neurological disorders, bone disorders, muscle disorders, vision disorders, speech disorders and hearing disorders are dismantled now and shall never reside in my body or in any of my familial blood line. I declare the twelve systems in my body:

25

Integumentary system (skin, hair, nails, sweat and exocrine glands), Skeletal system (bones- supporting the body and its organs), Nervous system (brain, spinal cord, nerves [sensory]), Muscular system (muscles- enables movement with the skeletal system), Endocrine system (secretes hormones includes: pituitary gland, thyroid gland, pancreas, adrenal gland, testes and ovaries), Reproductive system, Immune/Lymphatic system, Digestive system, Urinary system, Respiratory system and the Cardiovascular system (heart and blood vessels) are all functioning as they were designed to function. Just as You Lord created twelve tribes of Israel and Jesus called twelve disciples to be with him, You created Your most prized creation in man and woman and breathed life in us with twelve systems which is Your divine, perfect and authoritative number that completes us and makes us whole (Luke 9:1). The number twelve can also represent God's Kingdom. We therefore have the Kingdom of God in us. I represent Your Kingdom and Your culture of Heaven here on earth. Therefore, I decree and declare all viruses, bacteria, fungus and parasites have no effect on me or my familial blood line. I decree and declare that we have immunity to colds, flu, pneumonia, all fungal, parasitic diseases and any sickness or disease. When Jesus gave His life on the cross He said it is finished. Therefore, all sin, sickness and disease is covered, finished and left at the cross. The blood of the Lamb finished the work. Hallelujah! I declare, "I shall not die, but live, and declare the works of the Lord" (Psalm 118:17). I speak aloud Your Word, "**IT IS FINISHED**" (John 19:30)! I decree it to be so, by the power given to me, by the infallible Holy Word of God, in Jesus name, Amen.

My ears are open to hear your voice. Speak Lord!

_____

_____

Date Prayer Request Released   Date Prayer Answered

_____   _____

PRAYER AGAINST MENTAL ILLNESS

Heavenly Father, I pray for a sound mind for myself and the body of Christ. I speak now the mind of Christ in me, all of my familial blood line and the body of Christ (1 Corinthians 2:16). I call out every demonic spirit that tries to trick or take over my mind, my familial blood line and the body of Christ. I speak, "God hath not given us the spirit of fear; but of power, and of love, and of a sound mind" (2 Timothy 1:7). Therefore, anything that is not the power of God, the love of God and the mind of Christ has come into my body or mind illegally and I call it out now. I will guard what I see, hear and do that no demon will ever have access to my body or mind. Lord Your Word says, "And be not conformed to this world: but be ye transformed by the renewing of your mind, that ye may prove what is that good, and acceptable, and perfect, will of God" (Romans 12:2). Therefore, I will continually renew my mind with the washing of the Word of God, meditation on the Word of God, praise and worship, fasting and prayer (Ephesians 5:26, Joshua 1:8, Psalm 1:2, Mathew 17:21). My mind is alert and free from distractions. I have **LASER SHARP FOCUS** on my destiny and purpose. Every mental disorder or disease of the mind is cast out by my word and the words and will of God. I declare Your Word, "whatsoever things are true, whatsoever things are honest, whatsoever things are just, whatsoever things are pure, whatsoever things are lovely, whatsoever things are of good report; if there be any virtue, and if there be any praise, think on these things. Those things, which ye have both learned, and received, and heard, and seen in me, do: and the God of peace shall be with you" (Philippians 4:8-9). I declare I have peace of mind because I think on the right things. Because I submit to God and resist the devil daily he flees from me (James 4:7). I declare that my nervous system and all chemicals in my body are functioning as they were designed to function. I decree and declare all seducing spirits that try to fill the minds of Your sons and daughters with confusion are cast to the pits of hell. I decree the minds of Your sons and daughters are healthy, whole and free from any disease. Father, we lay every mental illness, ever attack of the mind and every spirit that has entered by any means, at Your feet Jesus. Because You Lord are not a respecter of persons, as You did it for those in the Bible, You can do it now for Your sons and daughters who have a challenge with mental illness (Matthew 4:24, Acts 10:34). Therefore, I decree You Lord have given Your sons and daughters a fearless spirit, a sound mind, a mind free of illness, self-control, and the ability to think clearly and intelligently (2 Timothy 1:7). Father You have already overcome the world therefore, You have overcome all illnesses including mental illness (John 16:33). Thank You Lord for Your power, that is perfect and comes forth where Your sons and daughters are weak (2 Corinthians 12:9). I decree as unclean spirits roam around trying to find domicile, the sons and daughters of the Most High God are covered and shielded from any occupation (Luke 11:24). Therefore, that enemy finds no rest

in Jesus name. I decree it to be so, by the power given to me, by the infallible Holy Word of God, in Jesus name, Amen.
My ears are open to hear your voice. Speak Lord!

_____

_____

Date Prayer Request Released   Date Prayer Answered

_____   _____

PRAYER FOR A HEALTHY LIFESTYLE

Dear Heavenly Father, You have made Your people perfectly and have left Your guide for us to live healthy and the ability to live a long life. For Your Word says, "And God said, Behold, I have given You every herb bearing seed, which is upon the face of all the earth, and every tree, in the which is the fruit of a tree yielding seed; to You it shall be for meat. And to every beast of the earth, and to every fowl of the air, and to everything that creepeth upon the earth, wherein there is life, I have given every green herb for meat: and it was so" (Genesis 1:29-30). Father You also said what You made was good (Genesis 1:31). Therefore, I decree that Your people will make wise decisions on the food we eat, how it is prepared, how much and how often we eat. You have given Your people wisdom, knowledge and understanding to make intelligent decisions, to be involved in physical activity, what we ingest, our work habits, sleep and rest habits. Because we have the wisdom of the Lord we will take care of our temple and will make a vow to not harm Your dwelling place, which is our body. Therefore, I decree that we will not defile the Spirit of God within us with unhealthy habits such as smoking, drug use, over use of alcohol, gluttony which is a sin, nor will we cause physical harm to self (Proverbs 23:20-21). I decree that food will not be our God (Philippians 3:19). I decree that we will serve and worship the only True and Living God (Jeremiah 10:10, 2 Corinthians 6:16). Therefore, I decree our days shall be one hundred and twenty healthy and not feeble years (Genesis 6:3). We will learn of You Lord and use Your wisdom and rest as You did (Genesis 2:2-3, Exodus 20:8-10). For Lord Your Word commands Your people to work for six days and then rest (Exodus 20:8-10; 33:14, Mark 2:27-28). Therefore, I decree that we will not be over worked, stressed, abused or misused in our careers, businesses, ministries, recreations or homes. If we ever feel that we need to enter into the rest of the Lord, I decree that we will lay our cares at Your feet and receive Your rest (Mathew 11:28-30). Your Word declares a rest for the people of God and how we should be diligent in seeking such rest (Hebrews 4:9-11). Therefore, I decree a diligent pursuit of God's rest daily, that we may be restored, refreshed and regenerated to complete the destined will of God for our lives in health, strength and power. I decree it to be so, by the power given to me, by the infallible Holy Word of God, in Jesus name, Amen.

My ears are open to hear your voice. Speak Lord!

_____

_____

Date Prayer Request Released   Date Prayer Answered

_____   _____

34

PART III: PRAYERS FOR POWER

PRAYER TO RELEASE BLESSING

Dear Heavenly Father, because I am a tither and not a robber of God, I ask You to release Your blessings on me (Malachi 3:8). I decree that You will "open the windows of heaven and pour out blessings that I will not have room enough to receive" (Malachi 3:10). The riches or wealth that have been laid up I release now with the words of my mouth (Proverb 13:22). I decree and declare that I follow the commandments of God which releases the blessings of the Lord to seek me out and chase me down (Deuteronomy 28:1-2). By my obedience to God's Holy Word, I have released a blessing on me and the city in which I reside (Deuteronomy 28:3). The field or place in which I work is releasing blessings unto me now (Deuteronomy 28:3). Because of my obedience to You Lord and Your word, You are releasing blessings on my children and all the fruits of my labor (Deuteronomy 28:4-5). Wherever I go, blessings are commanded to come to me (Deuteronomy 28:6, 8). Everything that I think on that is of the Father, the things that I put my hands to accomplish, the ground that I decide to walk on have already been given the commandment to be blessed by the Almighty and Sovereign God (Deuteronomy 28:8). Because I walk in the ways of the Father, I am established and blessed of the Lord beyond measure (Deuteronomy 28:9, 11). Because I am obedient to God's Word, good treasure from Heaven is released now unto me (Deuteronomy 28:12). Because I follow the counsel of God and not the word of a sinner, God is releasing blessings to me "like a tree planted by the rivers of water" of abundance and causing whatever I do to prosper (Psalm 1:3). I decree **OVERFLOW, OVERFLOW, OVERFLOW** now in Jesus name! The abundance of the outpour from Heaven blesses me in levels which go from my ankles, to the knees and so great that I have to swim in (Ezekiel 47:1-23). I decree that my blessings are released from the north, south, east and west and overflow to my family and those that are connected to me. I am blessed to be a blessing and therefore, I seek out the blessings of the Lord through obedience, to bless the nations. I decree it to be so, by the power given to me, by the infallible Holy Word of God, in Jesus name, Amen.

My ears are open to hear your voice. Speak Lord!

_____

_____

Date Prayer Request Released   Date Prayer Answered

_____   _____

PRAYER FOR MENTORS

Dear Heavenly Father, thank You for sending the ultimate sacrifice, Jesus Christ, to be the example to Your sons and daughters on how to live, act, speak and to lead others according to Your Word (John 13:13). Your Word declares, "If I then, your Lord and Master, have washed your feet; ye also ought to wash one another's feet. For I have given you an example, that ye should do as I have done to you"(John 13:14-15). Therefore, I ask Father that You select successors in the Land so that Your people will not be without examples or ensamples. You chose Joshua to follow Moses and lead Your chosen people to a promised land (Numbers 27:16-23). You chose Elisha to be mentored by Elijah (1 Kings 19:19). Therefore, Lord appoint my mentor. May my mentor transfer the double portion anointed mantle of God to me (2 Kings 2:1-15). May the mentor leadership spirit be so great that we resemble and long to be with each other to learn and grow (2 Kings 2:1-15). May my mentor sharpen me as Your Word declares, "Iron sharpeneth iron; so a man sharpeneth the countenance of his friend" (Proverbs 27:17). I declare that You teach me, O Lord, to be wise and to increase in learning (Proverbs 9:9). I declare that my ears are in tune to Your divine instruction (Proverbs 1:5). I thank You Father for Your comforter "which is the Holy Ghost, whom the Father will send in my name, he shall teach you all things, and bring all things to your remembrance, whatsoever I have said unto you" (John 14:26). Because wisdom comes from the Lord, I will not follow nor will I take counsel from the unlearned, ungodly or unwise (Proverbs 13:20). For Your Word says, "Blessed is the man that walketh not in the counsel of the ungodly, nor standeth in the way of sinners, nor sitteth in the seat of the scornful" (Psalms 1:1). Because I am obedient to Your Word, my spirit is open to receive the intelligence of the Lord. Therefore, whatsoever I put my mind to do shall prosper (Psalms 1:3). I decree God filled mentors are chasing Your sons and daughters down as blessings do because they see untapped potential. I decree it to be so, by the power given to me, by the infallible Holy Word of God, in Jesus name, Amen.

My ears are open to hear your voice. Speak Lord!

_____

_____

Date Prayer Request Released   Date Prayer Answered

_____   _____

PRAYER FOR FIVE FOLD MINISTERS

Heavenly Father, I declare that all pastors are called by You and have the integrity of the Lord. I pray Lord that You give pastors the ability to "know well the condition of their flock" entrusted to them (Proverbs 27:23). I decree Your purpose for the lives of the fivefold ministers will not be foiled, delayed, denied or frustrated. I pray that each minister of the gospel of Jesus has a heart of God and love the people of God. Our plan is Your plan. Our ears are Your ears and therefore we only say what we hear from the Father. We have an ear to hear what the Father is saying. We wait with anticipation and expectation what the Father will say. We know the voice of God and the voice of a stranger we will not follow (John 10:27, 10:5). Our mouth is Your mouth Lord, and therefore, we only say what You say. We minister Your Word and edify Your people. We will not abuse or misuse Your people entrusted to us. The finances and operation of every church and all affiliated businesses are cared for with integrity at all times. We carry the Kingdom mandate wherever we go. We are ambassadors to the throne of grace and therefore handle the Kingdom mandate with integrity, dignity, and honor. We will not dishonor any mantle placed upon us. We will guard the Kingdom and the mantle given to us. We will remain faithful to God and to the mantle given to us. We take care in planning, preparing and spending time at Jesus' feet. Each office that You have formed is important to the body of Christ and therefore, we will take special care to operate in our respective areas of anointing and ordination. Father, You said, "The harvest truly is great, but the labourers are few" (Luke 10:2). Therefore, I call forth apostles, prophets, pastors, evangelists and teachers to come forth, receive your mantles and operate with power in the world. I pray that the original design for the church to function under the apostolic anointing will manifest (1 Corinthians 12:28, Ephesians 4:11-12). Our churches will function with power because we follow Your mandate which states, "And God hath set some in the church, first apostles, secondarily prophets, thirdly teachers, after that miracles, then gifts of healings, helps, governments, diversities of tongues" (1 Corinthians 12:28). Therefore, we will operate at full capacity because we are obedient and operate all offices according to the Word of God. We have the results with the manifestation of signs, wonders, miracles and full throttle power because everyone is in their rightful place and in operation. I confess that every leader rules their house well, not controlled by any chemical substance, fleshly desires and is faithful to their spouse. I pray that each leader has time for their family and nothing is lacking, missing or broken. I declare that each minister's family is strong, loving and thriving. I dispel the name put on minister's children. Our children have a good name because they are taught of the Lord and do the right thing. I decree it to be so, by the power given to me, by the infallible Holy Word of God, in Jesus name, Amen.

My ears are open to hear your voice. Speak Lord!

_____

_____

Date Prayer Request Released   Date Prayer Answered

_____   _____

PRAYER TO RELEASE MANTLES

Heavenly Father You created me with purpose and destiny in mind. Therefore, I decree and declare that the mantle of authority and power that is necessary for my mission, be released unto me now. Release Your power, authority and wisdom into me now Lord. I pray for impartation of Your Glory, power, wisdom, eloquence and vigor. Father God do a new thing. Give me a new mantle that will manifest new levels of Glory, signs, wonders and miracles like never before. Father, just as Elisha was working and You allowed Elijah to come to seek him out and place a mantle of position on him, I declare You are doing the same for me (1 Kings 19:19). Now Lord anoint me with fresh oil to do Your will and work on earth to fulfill the mandate of Heaven. I decree and declare that I receive every mantle that You have for me. Hence, I receive the mantle that Jesus left when he said, "Verily, verily, I say unto you, He that believeth on me, **the works that I do shall he do also**; **and GREATER WORKS than these shall he do**; because I go unto my Father" (John 14:12). Therefore, I am busy doing the work of You Lord God. That which I hear the Father say to do that is what I will do. Let Your mantle of authority be so heavy that it is visible to others and compels them to follow Christ. Just as Elisha was present to see his mantle fall and was able to pick up the mantle and in double measure accomplish what his mentor did, I do the same (2 Kings 2:13-14). I am in the position to receive my mantle. I operate as Jesus operated and more while here on earth. I thank You that Your mantle is abundantly clear to me that I never have to wonder or operate under another's mantle. I thank You that the mantle of God upon me carries out the great commission. I thank You that my mantle gives me favor among all nations, kings, ambassadors, presidents, all dignitaries and opens doors that I may walk right in, unhindered. I thank You that there are new levels of Kingdom manifestation with my mantle. May I represent the Kingdom of God well with the kingdom mantle that has been placed upon me. Do a new thing Lord. My mantle is used to ignite people to move out of mediocrity into a place of Sovereignty. I move with the Glory cloud because it keeps me in tune with the movements of God. My mantle seats me in heavenly places like Moses, Peter, James, and John to receive downloads from the Father Himself (Exodus 33:21-23, 34:2-3, 5-6; Mathew 7:1-3). I represent my mantle and platform given to me with honor, humility, and integrity so that it will never bring shame to You, God. I decree it to be so, by the power given to me, by the infallible Holy Word of God, in Jesus name, Amen.

My ears are open to hear your voice. Speak Lord!

_____

_____

Date Prayer Request Released   Date Prayer Answered

_____   _____

PRAYER TO WALK IN MY PURPOSE

Dear Heavenly Father, it is my prayer that You would open the eyes of my understanding that I may know the reason You created me. I decree Your Word that You left for Adam and all creation to have dominion over every living creature on the earth and multiply. I decree and declare that You have left Your imprint in me that is just like You in creativity, power, authority, leadership and Glory. Therefore, I create things because I was born to be creative. I am a leader because I was born to lead and blaze trails. I was born with power because my Almighty Father in Heaven made me in His image and likeness. I decree that I am fearfully and wonderfully made by Elohim Re'Shiyth (Ra-Sheth) the God of the beginning (Genesis 1:1, Strong# H430, H7225). Before You created me in my mother's womb You had a purpose and destiny in mind and therefore, because I was birthed in this world, in this generation You have destined me with a specific purpose in mind (Jeremiah 29:11) You chose me to provide something to this world in this generation for an appointed time (Habakkuk 2:3). I declare Your Word, "for those whom He foreknew, He also predestined to become conformed to the image of His Son..."(Romans 8:29). Thank You, Lord, for not just creating me, but You also destined me for greatness. I decree I know my purpose because Your Word declares, "Ye are the light of the world. A city that is set on an hill cannot be hid... Let your light so shine before men, that they may see your good works, and glorify your Father which is in heaven" (Matthew 5:14-16). Because I walk in my purpose and calling the light of God is shining brightly that all can see. Men, women, boys and girls follow the light of God within me, they seek the Father and that same anointing light within me is sought for them. I am confident in what I was born and called to do. Therefore, the voice of a stranger I will not follow (John 10:5). Things that will not profit the Kingdom of God will not take my focus off of my Kingdom assignment. My purpose is to serve You with my hands, mouth, feet, heart, my service, using my gifts, talents and to worship You all the days of my life. For my body is and will always be a living sacrifice (Romans 12:1). When You created me in Your image and likeness You had increase, growth, development and the advancement of nations in mind. Abba Father, Adonai Asah (A-sa), God My Maker, You had territories mapped out for my use for the enhancement and furtherance of the Kingdom of God (Psalm 95:6, Strong# H6213). Father, I cast out fear, doubt and unbelief concerning my calling and destiny (Mathew 21:21, Luke 24:37-38, James 1:6, Mark 9:24; 11:23 John 20:27). I decree and declare that many mighty acts, miracles, signs, wonders and works manifest because of my belief (Mathew 13:58,1 Corinthians 12:28). I decree it to be so, by the power given to me, by the infallible Holy Word of God, in Jesus name, Amen.

My ears are open to hear your voice. Speak Lord!

_____

_____

Date Prayer Request Released   Date Prayer Answered

_____   _____

PRAYER FOR THE USE AND PERFECTION OF SPIRITUAL GIFTS

Dear Heavenly Father, I thank You for my spiritual gifts. I thank You for Your wisdom in the parable of the talents (Matthew 25: 14-30). I decree that the gifts that You have given me will be in full operation under the unction of the Holy Spirit and will not be buried. Father Your Word says, "Well done, good and faithful servant; thou hast been faithful over a few things, I will make thee ruler over many things: enter thou into the joy of thy lord" (Matthew 25:23). Therefore, I declare because I am faithful with the gift You have given me, You release even more abundant gifts to me (Mathew 25:28). I thank You that my gifts will be stirred by the washing of Your Word, meditation, prayer and being around others that have similar gifts. I seek out mentorship to help guide me in my spiritual gifts. For Your Word says, "If any of you lack wisdom, let him ask of God, that giveth to all men liberally, and upbraideth not; and it shall be given him" (James 1:5). Therefore, Lord I ask for wisdom in utilizing the gifts that You have given me. I decree and declare that spiritual gifts are given to me to use for the benefit of the church body (1 Corinthians 12:7). I decree that I work in harmony with my brothers and sisters in Christ with their spiritual gifts so that when we operate together, there is a synergistic effect that helps the body of Christ and advances the Kingdom. I decree that I will not abuse any spiritual gifts given to me nor will I abuse the people of God. I decree that my circles of influence are those that will motivate and push me to exercise my gifts to their full potential. I am in the right atmosphere to utilize my gifts. God graciously gives good gifts to me because I ask for them. I receive Your gifts with open arms and an open heart. I denounce the pride of thinking the gifts of God are of my own power. I decree that lives are saved, healed, delivered and made the better because of my gifts and their connection to me. I decree it to be so, by the power given to me, by the infallible Holy Word of God, in Jesus name, Amen.

My ears are open to hear your voice. Speak Lord!

_____

_____

Date Prayer Request Released   Date Prayer Answered

_____   _____

PART IV: SPIRITUAL WARFARE PRAYERS

PRAYER TO RELEASE POWER OVER DEMONS IN THE MARKETPLACE

Heavenly Father, by the power given to me by Your Word, I decree and declare that my workplace shall be Holy. I set the atmosphere by the power given to me by Your Word. I call out every demon that has illegally planted themselves in my coworkers, in the administrators, in the parking lot of my workplace and in the cracks and crevices of the building of my workplace. As I walk on the foundation of my workplace, I command every demon to leave now. Every curse that was spoken or thought I decree that curse is dismantled, foiled, and utterly destroyed now. Every assignment that is designed to frustrate me or Your purpose for me God, I cancel now by the power of God's Holy Word that was given to me. Father God I ask that You will send Your Holy Spirit to give me the appropriate, anointed, and powerful words to speak when trouble may come my way. Bridle my tongue when it needs to be bridled. I cast down every stronghold that tries to take authority over me in the workplace. All unclean spirits are illegal and therefore I call you back to the pits of hell where you belong. God Your Word says, "For we wrestle not against flesh and blood, but against principalities, against powers, against the rulers of the darkness of this world, against spiritual wickedness in high places" (Ephesians 6:12). Therefore, I put on the whole armor of God that I will withstand the wiles of the devil (Ephesians 6:11). I decree that my faith in Your Word God will quench every fiery dart that is launched at me. I declare that I have "power to tread on serpents and scorpions, and over all the power of the enemy: and nothing shall by any means hurt me" (Luke 10:19). Therefore, I dismantle every diabolical weapon, contract, assignment, plot, plan, ploy, scheme, and device of the enemy against my life. Frustrate the enemy's purpose against me. Confound the enemy's plans and communication against me. I decree it to be so, by the power given to me, by the infallible Holy Word of God, in Jesus name, Amen.

My ears are open to hear your voice. Speak Lord!

_____

_____

Date Prayer Request Released   Date Prayer Answered

_____   _____

PRAYER AGAINST SEXUAL ADDICTIONS

Father God, I cry out for Your people, who may be struggling with the sin of sex outside of marriage. I stand in the gap for Your people and decree that we offer up our bodies as living sacrifices to God, our creator (Romans 12:1). I decree that we are not persuaded by this world to have sex. We keep our eyes looking straight towards the mark of Your calling on our lives. I confess that we decide to look upon only those things that are pleasing to God and those things that bring our flesh under subjection to the Word of God and not manipulate us to fall. I decree there is no pressure from the world to sleep with the same sex, opposite sex, to use sex toys or partake in masturbation. Those things mentioned are of this world and not of God. Therefore, I bind up even the thought to participate in any act that will manipulate our thoughts, mind, and body to do anything outside of the will of God. I decree that our mind is free and clear of any images or acts that have been performed in the past. I decree and declare that our mind has no recollection of any previous ungodly acts or thoughts. I confess a renewed mind right now by the blood of the Lamb (Romans 12:2). Father God, help all those that are struggling with sexual addictions live a pure, Holy and God-filled life. I decree and declare that those who are not married will pray for a Godly mate to come into their lives, so they can be intimate with their spouse. Father Your Word says, "For the wages of sin is death; but the gift of God is eternal life through Jesus Christ our Lord" (Romans 6:23). Therefore, I confess that we study the Word of God and commit it to memory so that we will not sin against You God and accept Christ that we may live and have eternal life. I confess that we yield ourselves to You God and not to sin (Romans 6:13). I shout out loud so that joker, the devil, hears loud and clear, "sin shall not have dominion over [me]: for [I am] not under the law, but under grace" (Romans 6:14). I confess those struggling with sexual addiction are delivered and set free and no remnants of thoughts of the acts remain. I decree my family, friends and connections are free from sexual addictions. I decree there is a pressing in the Spirit to reach for the deeper things of God and for the purpose and destiny for our lives (Philippians 3:13-14, Luke 5:4). No longer are we satisfied by the flesh, but satisfied only by the Spirit, presence, and leading of God. I speak against every attack of the enemy to lure us into repeated immoral acts of the flesh. I confess that our body is the temple of the Holy Spirit (1 Corinthians 6:19). Because the Spirit of God will not dwell in an unclean temple, we diligently refrain from unlawful sexual desires, sexual paraphernalia, sexual content on television, movies, places and people that are connected to lasciviousness. I declare we are bought with a high price by the blood of Jesus. Therefore, I declare we will "glorify God in our bodies and in our spirit which all belongs to God" (1 Corinthians 6:20). Satan, take your hand off of God's people now! Sexual addiction has no hold on Gods people. I decree it to be so, by the power given to me, by the infallible Holy Word of God, in Jesus name, Amen.

My ears are open to hear your voice. Speak Lord!

_____

_____

Date Prayer Request Released   Date Prayer Answered

_____   _____

PRAYER AGAINST CHEMICAL ADDICTIONS

Heavenly Father Your Word declares, "For all that is in the world, the lust of the flesh, and the lust of the eyes, and the pride of life, is not of the Father, but is of the world" (1John 2:16). Therefore, I declare I will not follow the ways of this world nor will I pleasure my flesh with the seducing spirits of this world but I will follow the ways of the Lord (Psalm 18:30, Isaiah 55:8, Psalm 37:5). I decree that Your Word says that I am free and who the Son sets free is free indeed. I cry out to You Lord and I know You will answer because Your Word says, "call upon me in the day of trouble: I will deliver thee and thou shall glorify me" (Psalm 50:15). Help O Lord that I may glorify You. Father God I surrender my life to You and ask for forgiveness and total healing from all chemicals that hinder or alter my mind from making any rational, intelligent decisions. Father, Your Word says that my sins are as far as the east is from the west and You remember my sins no more (Psalm 103:12). So Father, I humbly come to You asking that You forgive my choices and actions and heal my body from the taste, smell or desire for any chemical that is not of You. Take the wheel Abba Father. I can do nothing in my own power but only in Your strength and power. I decree that I will no longer make a chemical, substance, object or person my idol, but I only serve You today and forevermore. I bow down to You Lord and release at the feet of Jesus, all of the things that hold me back from being the best that You have called me to be. I decree that the temptations of this world no longer have a hold on me. I shout out, "**no weapon that is formed against me will ever prosper**" (Isaiah 54:17)! I declare, "Every defile tongue that tries to rise against me will never manifest itself for this is my heritage from my God" (Isaiah 54:17). I decree that the weapons that were given to me "are not carnal, but mighty through God to the pulling down of strongholds" (2 Corinthians 10:4). Therefore, every stronghold is broken and no longer has a hold on me. Because I have the Holy Spirit I am comforted in the difficult times. I decree that all chemical demonic assignments that have attached to me are uprooted, canceled and cast to the pits of hell. I declare that I am a new creature and old habits, friends in that spirit of influence, old hangouts, old paradigms and old desires have passed away (2 Corinthians 5:17). I am fully delivered from any destructive spirits in the name of Jesus. The blood of the Lamb of the Most High God covers me from all unrighteousness and protects me from further debilitating addicting spirits (1John 1:17). Now that I am free I decree that I will not "submit again to the yoke of slavery" (Galatians 5:1). I "Put to death therefore what is earthly in [me]: sexual immorality, impurity, passion, evil desire, and covetousness, which is idolatry" (Colossians 3:5). Lord as I present my body as a living sacrifice unto You, may You receive me with open arms (Romans 12:1). I decree it to be so, by the power given to me, by the infallible Holy Word of God, in Jesus name, Amen.

My ears are open to hear your voice. Speak Lord!

_____

_____

Date Prayer Request Released   Date Prayer Answered

_____   _____

PRAYER AGAINST SUICIDE

Abba Father, I stand against premature death of Your sons and daughters (Ecclesiastes 7:17). Because Your Holy Spirit dwells within Your people, I declare that we shall protect Your vessel (1 Corinthians 3:16-17, 1 Corinthians 6:19-20). I declare Your Holy spirit is there to lead and guide us in the way that we should go and we, therefore, will protect the heavenly gift within us (John 16:13). I cancel every assignment of the evil spirits of low self-esteem, low self-worth, despair, hopelessness, hallucinations, voices from the enemy, depression, and suicide. I declare that we have a hunger and a thirst to find that perfect will for our lives. I decree due diligence to discover the plans that You have for our lives. For Your Word declares that You Lord, the Most High God (El Elyon) knows the plans You have for us (Jeremiah 1:5). No matter what it looks or feels like, we trust You. For You did not create us for sudden calamity or destruction. Your Word declares, "I know the thoughts that I think toward you, saith the LORD, thoughts of peace, and not of evil, to give you an expected end" (Jeremiah 29:11). Therefore, my end has already been determined by God and not by my hands. I decree that You Lord have placed destiny, the desire to live, abundant life, purpose and a call to action in this world. Therefore, there is no self-pity or frustration in the process of me fulfilling my purpose. I decree and declare the choice of Your people is life and not death, to declare the works of the Lord (Deuteronomy

30:19). Father, we call out to You when we have feelings that do not line up with Your Word. Your Word declares that we can call on You and You will answer (Isaiah 58:9, Psalm 91:15, Jeremiah 29:12, Jeremiah 33:3). Father hear our cry (Psalm 39:12). Hear our plea (Psalm 39:12). We need the comforter to comfort us and to pull us out of the pit. I decree and declare, Your Words will I hide in my heart that I may never sin against You. Therefore, we will speak Your Word daily and in every situation that we may find ourselves in (1 Peter 4:11, Proverbs 15:4). I declare that if I lose anything of value, I still have Jesus and that is enough to start all over again. I declare that there is nothing too hard for our Master (Jeremiah 32:27, Luke 18:27). Therefore, whatever has been holding us back, no longer has a hold on Your people. Enemy of the Lord, loose us and let us go now in Jesus name! Father help Your sons and daughters to see ourselves as You see us. You call us a peculiar people and a royal priesthood (1 Peter 2:9). Help us to not think or believe negative thoughts. To protect the minds of Your people, things that are pure, good report and of virtue are things that we think on. We declare Your Word daily. We commit Your Word to memory as we meditate on Your Word day and night (Psalm 1:2). We choose to only believe Your report of us. I decree the weapon of the Lord is mighty and we use it daily to pull down every stronghold of words spoken or deeds done towards us (2 Corinthians 10:4). Your Word declares that our weapons are "Casting down imaginations, and every high thing that exalts itself against the knowledge of God, and bringing into captivity every thought to the obedience of Christ" (2 Corinthians 10:5). Therefore, every evil or counterproductive thought that tries to come in the minds of Your sons and daughters is annihilated by the Word of God. I declare that we push out every evil thought with thoughts of God and meditation on His Word. I decree and declare that Your sons and daughters follow Your principal to submit to You Lord and resist the thoughts and actions of the devil. Therefore, Satan will certainly flee because he has nothing to work with (James 4:7). I shout out loud, we are free from the thoughts and acts of suicide! I decree it to be so, by the power given to me, by the infallible Holy Word of God, in Jesus name, Amen.

My ears are open to hear your voice. Speak Lord!

_____

_____

Date Prayer Request Released   Date Prayer Answered

_____   _____

PRAYER AGAINST ABUSE

Dear Heavenly Father, I seek You on behalf of all those who are being abused, those that have been abused in the past, misused, manipulated or taken advantage of. I decree and declare that all those involved in any form of abuse, controlling or manipulative behaviors will cease now. I decree that the hand of God is on all those involved in mistreating God's people. I speak to those who have been abusing God's people. You will abuse no more! I shout aloud, "Satan, The Lord rebuke thee" (Zechariah 3:2)! I declare those who have been hurt in the past will not turn and be abusers themselves. I declare vengeance is the Lords (Deuteronomy 32:35). Therefore, we will not take revenge for ourselves (Romans 12:19). Your Word says, " But I say unto you, Love your enemies, bless them that curse you, do good to them that hate you, and pray for them which despitefully use you, and persecute you; That ye may be the children of your Father which is in heaven: for he maketh his sun to rise on the evil and on the good, and sendeth rain on the just and on the unjust" (Matthew 5:44-45). I decree that all of those abused and even the abuser are set free from all thoughts, visions, acts or deeds of old (John 8:36). Who the Son makes free is free indeed (John 8:36). Lord Your word declares, "Let all bitterness, and wrath, and anger, and clamour, and evil speaking, be put away from you, with all malice: And be ye kind one to another, tenderhearted, forgiving one another, even as God for Christ's sake hath forgiven you" (Ephesians 4:31-32). Your Word also communicates that we can be angry but sin not. Therefore, we will strive to be at peace with all people. I speak against every evil spirit that is behind the spirit of anger, bitterness, wrath, abuse and misuse. For Your Word declares, "But now ye also put off all these; anger, wrath, malice, blasphemy, filthy communication out of your mouth (Colossians 3:8). I declare anger and hate is away from our lips and is therefore not a part of our spirits and is far from us. I declare the blood of the Lamb covers Your children so that no harm will ever come near (Exodus 12:13, Psalm 91:10-14, Revelation 12:11). At the onset of trouble, Your name Lord, will we cry aloud and You Lord will hear and deliver us (Psalm 91:15-16). EL GIBBOR, Mighty God, God of Strength, God of Power, Warrior, and Champion "fight against them that fight against [us]" (Psalm 35:1). For JEHOVAH NISSI, You are the Banner and the God of Victory (Exodus 17:15). This is a fixed fight against the spirits of darkness. Therefore, we always win. I speak against premature death, broken bones, bruises, brain damage, loss of any kind and emotional breakdowns from any abusive relationship or connection in any way. I decree that anyone involved in this situation gets the revelation of their worth and receives the wisdom and financial resources to leave any abusive situation. I decree there are no emotional ties with the enemy. Therefore, there is no desire to return to any toxic situations. I decree there are divine supernatural connections that speak the Word of God and edify those abused, that they now have a support system that will not allow anyone in that situation to look back. I decree it to be so, by the power given to me, by the infallible Holy Word of God, in Jesus name, Amen. My ears are open to hear your voice. Speak Lord!

_____

_____

Date Prayer Request Released   Date Prayer Answered

_____   _____

PRAYER AGAINST THE SPIRIT OF JEZEBEL

Abba Father I decree that we are free and have no open doors for Satan and his evil spirits, including the Jezebel spirit, to have access to Your people. Everything that the spirit of Jezebel represents: manipulation, arrogance, demeaning, boastful, coercion, idolatry, control, murder, seduction, cunning, divisive, cruel, liars, secretive, disregard to protocol or rules, threatening, I denounce now in Jesus name. Father, this spirit has been known to discreetly come in and cause the destruction of marriages, churches, friendship, families, and businesses. Therefore, I decree and declare that no spirit will ever cause division in our families, friendships, ministries or businesses because the blood of the Lamb covers Your children. I decree the gift of discernment over Your people to detect this evil spirit and speak out against this spirit and call it out from the premises of the dwelling places of your children (1 John 4:1-3). I declare there will be no destruction of Your people by this spirit because we serve the true and Living God and Your hand Father is upon Your children and ready to remove the enemy before destruction can take place. Every plot and scheme of the spirit of Jezebel is foiled, frustrated and annihilated at the root of conception. The blood is against the spirit of Jezebel. I decree the spirit of Jezebel and all affiliated spirits go back to the pits of hell. The Word of God declares that we, as disciples, have authority and dominion over unclean spirits (Mathews 10:1). Therefore, I decree that whatever we decree shall be established because Your Word also declares we shall have what we say (Mark 11:24). We decree your Word with power, force and authority because we have power in our tongue (Proverbs 18:21). Father God, I renounce every association with a Jezebel spirit. Jehovah Gibbor, Mighty God, fight and break up all evil connections that try to attack Your children (Isaiah 9:6). I now declare Your Word, I bind up the spirit of Jezebel and all associated spirits (Mathew 18:18). No longer Jezebel, will you have your way in God's churches, families, marriages, music, media, relationships, political seats, cities, states, and nations. God's people rise up now, put on the whole armor of God and take the sword of the Spirit and annihilate this seducing cunning spirit (Ephesians 6:10-20). I speak frustration and confusion to the spirit of Jezebel. I command that foul spirit to be forced into the pits of hell now in Jesus name. To hell, you evil spirit that seduces same-sex relationships and tricks them away from the commands of God. To hell, you foul spirit that seduces men and women to live based on how they feel and not by the Word of God. To hell, you foul spirit that seduces same-sex relationships and marriages that decrease procreation. To hell, you foul spirit that seduces the minds of God's people to kill. No devious or defiant Jezebel spirit will ever be allowed to whisper innuendos that do not line up with the Word of God. I decree God's children know His voice; we listen intently in expectation for the Rhema Word from God. Therefore, the voice of a stranger we will not follow (John 10:5). I decree and declare the things that have been tolerated from the spirit of Jezebel and its associated spirits are no longer tolerated or welcomed in the Kingdom of God. I decree it to be so, by the power given to me, by the infallible Holy Word of God, in Jesus name, Amen.

My ears are open to hear your voice. Speak Lord!

_____

_____

Date Prayer Request Released   Date Prayer Answered

_____   _____

PRAYER AGAINST PORNOGRAPHY

Heavenly Father I decree the purity of Your people. I decree the filth that the enemy has brought into this world as a plot to lure the women and men of God into sin is canceled and placed in the pits of hell (Proverbs 6:24-26, 7:21-27, 1 John 2:16, Matthew 5:28, Galatians 5:19). Pornography is a sin. We know the sneakiness of the enemy to entice and ensnare God's sons and daughters into sin. Your Word declares, "Every man is tempted, when he is drawn away of his own lust, and enticed. Then when lust hath conceived, it bringeth forth sin: and sin, when it is finished, bringeth forth death (James 1:14-15). Therefore, I cancel the thought that the enemy has placed in the minds of God's people that pornography is harmless and allows a person to release stress or sexual frustration. I stand against the things that it has brought to the minds of people in the form of masturbation, sex toys and anything else that perverts how intimacy should be used as designed by God; to be in a marriage between one man and one woman, who have given themselves to marriage in the presence of God (Genesis 1:28, 2:18, 21-25). I speak against pornography as it has been a sneaky gateway to child abuse, trafficking, abuse, adultery, sodomy, homosexuality and so much more. I cancel every sex store, the sex industry, porn star, every studio, home, set; the location where movies are produced is canceled. Frustrate the purpose and plans of this foul and lustful spirit. Dry up the resources that funnel into any part of pornography production. Even cancel every amateur production of pornography. Cleanse the minds, eyes, ears, and souls that have been subjected in the past to any form of pornography. May they remember no more. Your Word says if we confess our faults and ask for forgiveness You will forgive us and remember our sins no more (Micah 7:19, Jeremiah 31:34, Hebrews 8:12, 10:17, Isaiah 1:18, 43:25, 44:22, Acts 3:19). I decree, "As far as the east is from the west, so far hath he removed our transgressions from us" (Psalm103:12). Write your laws on our minds and place them in our hearts that we may never sin against You (Hebrews 10:16). We now make a covenant with our eyes and bodies that we will not look at pornography or take part in any form of lustful acts that proceed from pornography or any parts of this industry (Job 31:1). Our bodies are living sacrifices and should be presented to the Most High God as Holy (Romans 12:1-2). We awake O Lord and expose and bring to light, all that the enemy is doing to pull Your people into darkness (Ephesians 5:11-14). We are the light of the world and therefore, our actions will never have to be hidden because we are obedient to the Word of God. The camp of the enemy has been infiltrated by the armies of the Kingdom of God. The ground of the enemy has been turned over and cast into the pits of hell. I decree and declare we love to please God, therefore; we will not participate in unfruitful ways and things that do not profit the Kingdom of God. I decree it to be so, by the power given to me, by the infallible Holy Word of God, in Jesus name, Amen.

My ears are open to hear your voice. Speak Lord!

_____

_____

Date Prayer Request Released   Date Prayer Answered

_____   _____

PRAYER AGAINST HUMAN & SEX TRAFFICKING

Dear Heavenly Father, I speak out against the plans of the enemy to hold captive, keep in bondage and keep a yoke over the necks of Your people. I decree that the enemy will loose every man, woman, girl and boy that are held to be used in any immoral sex act, selling of young children for marriage, slaves, and abuse. I declare the enemy loose them now, release them now and let them go now in Jesus name! I pray that no one takes an interest in buying any human for any sex act, adolescent marriage or slaves. I ask Father that You would give Your wisdom and power to every person that may come in contact with anyone that tries to coerce, manipulate or demand the use of their services illegally. I decree that every road, flight, train, bus, car, van, boat, route of transfer, is frustrated, blocked, shut down and nontransferable. Help Your people financially Lord, that they are not persuaded to sell family members to live. Feed Your people Lord. Send Your loving people into the field to provide the Word of God, the love of God, the peace of God, financial assistance, educational assistance and any physical need necessary for survival. Your Word declares, "There is nothing new under the sun" just things manipulated to seem new (Ecclesiastes 1:9). Therefore, whatever the enemy has thought, You already had a solution for it. The enemy can no longer hide because the light of God shines in the dark places (Luke 8:17, 1 Corinthians 4:5). Therefore, I decree that the people who are being used of the enemy receive the Word of God somehow, in some way, maybe by television, radio, sign, book, magazine or person that convicts them to loose the captives, turn and receive God in their hearts. For all those involved with these inhumane acts, I decree wire transfers, bank accounts, offshore accounts and monies laid up is blocked, canceled and destroyed now in Jesus name. Frustrate and confound the enemy's purpose. I pray that those released from bondage and those released from being the aggressor will go back and help others, form and assist with a task force with local and global authorities, produce programs to prevent and release those in sex or human trafficking. I decree counseling services to help restore those affected and a method devised to reunite families together. I declare that those who have been seduced into this lifestyle is free. Jesus declares, "If the Son therefore shall make you free, ye shall be free indeed" (John 8:36). We are free! We are free! We are free in Jesus name. I declare, "There is nothing too hard for God" (Jeremiah 32:27, Genesis 18:14, Luke 18:27). Therefore, I declare that the business of sex and human trafficking is no longer lucrative. I command sex and human trafficking cease now. I decree it to be so, by the power given to me, by the infallible Holy Word of God, in Jesus name, Amen.

My ears are open to hear your voice. Speak Lord!

82

Date Prayer Request Released   Date Prayer Answered

_____   _____

PRAYER AGAINST DRUG TRAFFICKING

Dear Heavenly Father, pour out Your spirit on every border, every coastline, every highway, every airline terminal, train terminal, bus terminal and any other means by which drugs, guns and illegal paraphernalia, attempt to enter into Your nations. I declare that every satanic portal that has been open up to now is closed in Jesus name. Therefore, every means of making drugs, money portal, all machinery used to measure drugs, weapons, dogs, people that produce, funnel, traffic, and protect drugs is shut down now in Jesus name. Satan, the Lord rebuke you and all your evil attempts, plots, plans and schemes to corrupt and ultimately kill God's sons and daughters (Zechariah 3:2). Father, I declare that every dollar is dried up from the pockets of every person involved in drug and gun traffic practice. I declare the salvation of those who have been sucked in by Satan's plot to destroy mankind, by any means necessary. Those who have been seduced to take money from the bloodshed of God's people, I decree and declare your release from the grips of Satan now! I decree the hearts be turned toward God to love, worship, serve God alone and to turn from all wicked ways of all drug traffickers and all affiliated illegal practices. I declare that all nations and people are set free from drug trafficking, human trafficking, weapon trafficking and any illegal diabolical behaviors. Your Word declares, "If the Son therefore shall make you free, ye shall be free indeed" (John 8:36). I declare every woman, man, boy or girl involved in any of these diabolical behaviors get a revelation, meet Jesus, ask for forgiveness, turn from their wicked ways, accept Jesus as their Lord and Savior and live by the Word of God all the days of their lives. I decree because these drug traffickers have run this diabolical business they have now turned their knowledge of running such business into a legal business that not only creates wealth but brings Glory to God and wealth to the nations. I pray for the peace, comfort, and forgiveness of the families that have been affected by these diabolical, illegal practices. I decree and declare God's children that have been seduced to using illegal drugs are free from the taste of drugs and the lifestyle. I decree and declare that families are restored with love, joy and abundance of life. I decree neighborhoods, communities, states and countries are revitalized and taken back for the Glory of God. I decree it to be so, by the power given to me, by the infallible Holy Word of God, in Jesus name, Amen.

My ears are open to hear your voice. Speak Lord!

_____

_____

Date Prayer Request Released   Date Prayer Answered

_____   _____

PRAYER AGAINST SEX STORES, STRIP CLUBS, BROTHELS AND ALL AFFILIATED BUSINESSES AND PRODUCTS

Heavenly Father, I decree that my neighborhood, community, city, and state is free from all sex stores, strip clubs, brothels and all affiliated businesses and products. I speak out against the very grounds that immoral acts are done. The children of this world are no longer enticed by the perversion created by the enemy. The illusions of feeling good at all cost and anything goes is cursed at the root. Money is no longer funneled through the hands of God's people for any lascivious acts created by the hand of Satan. I declare sex trade, prostitution, pornography, those that participate in porn, sexual paraphernalia of all kinds, strip clubs, brothels and all affiliated places and things are no longer profitable. I declare that the enemy is frustrated and confounded that every person that was once alright with this life has now denounced it because they have found the Lord Jesus as their Savior and no longer are willing to participate in such sin. For the Word of God declares, "Know ye not that the unrighteous shall not inherit the kingdom of God? Be not deceived: neither fornicators, nor idolaters, nor adulterers, nor effeminate, nor abusers of themselves with mankind" (1 Corinthians 6:9). Therefore, I call out all of those drawn into this lifestyle and speak that they are now coming forth to worship the Lord God and denounce all unrighteousness. I condemn every building, the strip of land or place that operates with the sale of people, sexual favors of any kind, the sale of fantasy, sex toys, sex tapes, sex magazines, bondage, bestiality, sodomy, homosexuality, revealing of any body part that was designed to be revealed in marriage. Your word is clear, "For you may be sure of this, that everyone who is sexually immoral or impure, or who is covetous [that is, an idolater], has no inheritance in the kingdom of Christ and God" (Ephesians 5:5). Therefore, we will adhere to Your Word Lord so that we may receive our inheritance in the Kingdom of God. I decree it to be so, by the power given to me, by the infallible Holy Word of God, in Jesus name, Amen.

My ears are open to hear your voice. Speak Lord!

_____

_____

Date Prayer Request Released   Date Prayer Answered

_____   _____

PRAYER OVER MEDIA

Abba Father, I decree that Your children will not love the things of this world (1 John 2:15-17). The things that have been shown and released in the media will no longer be tolerated. I decree that Your children will no longer be lead astray by the media system of this world (Mathew 24:4, Ephesians 5:11). The enemy's time is up! I decree that the control of media has been reversed and turned into the hands of God's sons and daughters. Now that the media which includes: networks, radio, movie industry and all forms of communication are released in mass quantities to the nations, we reach out to You for Your direction and wisdom in the area of media. I decree that journalists, writers, producers, actors, actresses and all those involved in the decision-making process of what we, as consumers have available to watch and hear, are Christians and choose to only participate in things that bring Glory to God. I declare that what is allowed to go before our eyes and ears are prophetic words, the Word of God, edifying words, clean fun humor, encouragement, wisdom, knowledge, informative and loving information. Father give Your sons and daughters a hunger for truth, factual, beneficial, healthy, Christian, family structure as written by the Word of God and clean television, movies and radio. May entertainment be redefined by the people of God that media will not be a channel for violence, vulgarity, profanity, homosexuality, satanic worship, horror, nudity, lust and men and women falling short of the Glory of

God. I decree and declare the sons and daughters of the Most High God are leading in the media system of this world. We own networks, radio stations, newspapers, and magazines. The sons and daughters of God have decision-making authority in the Federal Communications Commission and national public radio. Now Father put a hedge of protection around the journalists and camera persons who extend themselves for the Glory of God to other nations for news coverage. May the journalists cover actual, factual and current events. May the media teams be granted full access to remote countries to be the eyes and ears for those who are not able to travel. Although the media teams are sent to cover news information, may You provide time for them to be used as Your representative to share the Gospel of Jesus Christ (Matthew 28:19, Ephesians 5:19-20). May the love of Christ and the Word of God spread abroad in all the world by the men and women of God chosen to represent Your Kingdom through media (Colossians 3:16). For media is a way to spread the Gospel around the world. Therefore, Lord of Host anoint the air waves and the pixels in every television or movie theater screen to show forth Your Kingdom. Manifest Your Glory to every nation through global networking. **Your nations Lord** are the better because Your Kingdom ambassadors are owners and leaders in the media system. I decree it to be so, by the power given to me, by the infallible Holy Word of God, in Jesus name, Amen.

My ears are open to hear your voice. Speak Lord!

_____

_____

Date Prayer Request Released   Date Prayer Answered

_____   _____

PRAYER AGAINST THE SPIRIT OF HEROD & PHARAOH
(ABORTION, DEVALUING LIFE, MURDER)

Abba Father, Adoni Asah (A-sa), the Lord our Maker, contend with those who contends with us and "fight against" those who "fight against" us (Psalm 95:6; 35:1, Strong# H6213). I demand the spirits of Herod, Pharaoh, premature death, murder, abortion and devaluing life to be cast into the depths of hell. I call out the spirits of Jezebel that works with other spirits such as Herod, Ahab, Pharaoh and the python spirit which is used to confuse the minds of God's people to make them think that they have the right to murder God's seed, purpose, and destiny. I decree and declare the cancellation of all plots and schemes against premature death and murder of God's people. To hell all of you foul spirits. You have no rights to God's people! I decree and declare God's fire ring of protection all around His people in Jesus name (Zechariah 2:5). I declare the horses and chariots of fire from the Kingdom of God protect us from all evil, unclean spirits (2 Kings 6:17). Blind the eyes of the enemy that it cannot locate Your people at any time (2 Kings 6:18). I decree that all signals or communication devices that lead to God's people, be shut down now. Frustrate and confound the purposes of these foul spirits. We suit up with the whole armor of God (Ephesians 6:10-20). We will not run scared at the decrees of this world because we know that our God protects His people just as He did for Moses (Exodus 2:1-

10). Even at the time when Pharaoh was killing all male babies born, God turned it around and allowed Moses to live (Exodus 1:8-22; 2:1-10, Romans 8:28). Moses traveled on the same river that Pharaoh ordered babies to be killed and thrown in (Exodus 1:22). Moses's own mother got paid to receive her baby back and feed him (Exodus 2:1-10). That's the kind of God we serve! I declare that Your seed Lord multiplies and replenishes the earth with God filled and Holy Spirit-filled children of the Most High God (Genesis 1:28, Exodus 1:7) El Gibbor, God Almighty, show Yourself strong and powerful over all these unclean spirits (Isaiah 9:6). I annihilate the spirit of Herod. That bullying spirit must die. I decree just as Jesus Christ was spared from the grips of Herod, so shall the sons and daughters of God be spared because we are heirs with Christ (Matthew 2:1-19). Every attempt to assassinate our dreams, visions, purpose and destiny is ambushed by the angels of God now (Psalm 91:10-12). We pull down every stronghold that the spirit of Herod, Pharaoh, Jezebel, Ahab, Python and any other unclean spirit who tries to attach itself to our lives (2 Corinthians 10:4-5). Unclean spirits you are outnumbered (Deuteronomy 32:30, Psalm 91:7). Unclean spirit your time is up! You are not welcome and must go back to the pits of hell! Unclean spirits, you are illegally trespassing on the earth that Adonai Asah, God the Creator and El Gibbor, God Almighty has given to His sons and daughters, to have dominion over (Genesis 1:28). I decree the python spirit will not choke the life out of God's children because the head of the python spirit has been cut off. Therefore, there is no more life in the python spirit. I decree it to be so, by the power given to me, by the infallible Holy Word of God, in Jesus name, Amen. My ears are open to hear your voice. Speak Lord!

_____

_____

Date Prayer Request Released   Date Prayer Answered

_____   _____

PRAYER AGAINST LEGAL MATTERS

Heavenly Father, I declare that Your sons and daughters will be obedient and adhere to Your Word, which is given as a guide for wisdom and a manual for living. Because Your sons and daughters adhere to Your Word, I decree there is a protective barrier from legal issues. I declare that illegal practices are far from us; therefore, we will not find ourselves in prison or frustrated by the legal system of this world. I decree peace among Your sons and daughters. For Your Word declares, "If it be possible, as much as lieth in you, live peaceably with all men (Romans 12:18). Because we live in this world, we know there will be legal matters. Therefore, Lord we ask You to be the Judge and jury. Let not the enemy get away with lies and deceit. We put it all in Your hands, for vengeance is Yours (Romans 12:19). Raise up witnesses in Your sons and daughters favor. I decree there will be no anxiety as to the outcome of the matter. For You, Father, work perfectly in impossibilities. Shaphat (Sha-fat), God our Judge, plead and judge our case (James 4:12, Judges 11:27, Strong# H8199). Father as Your sons and daughters are asked to open our mouths to plead our case, speak through us. I ask that Your Holy Spirit will bring to our remembrance the exact and actual facts of the matter (John 14:26). Father, Your Word declares, "Thou gavest also thy good spirit to instruct" (Nehemiah 9:20). Therefore, Shaphat, God our Judge, breathe Your ruwach (ru-akh), Your heavenly Spirit within us and speak on our behalf (Genesis

2:7, Strong# H7307). Empower Your sons and daughters to stand on the enemy's line and victoriously plead our case. Your Word declares we do not have to worry or even think about what we will say. Abba Father, Your Word declares, "For it is not ye that speak, but the Spirit of your Father which speaketh in you" (Matthew 10:20). Your sons and daughters Lord shout for victory now! The all-powerful, Almighty God is in control and has already determined that His children win! It is a fixed fight! We win! The things that have been taken from Your people is returned in excellent condition. Money that is owed is returned with interest. Properties are released back into the hands of Your sons and daughters Lord. Children are being reunited with the families of God. I decree it to be so, by the power given to me, by the infallible Holy Word of God, in Jesus name, Amen.

My ears are open to hear your voice. Speak Lord!

_____

_____

Date Prayer Request Released   Date Prayer Answered

_____   _____

PRAYER THAT ELIMINATES EXTREMIST GROUPS THAT DEVISE EVIL

Abba Father, we need Your power to defeat the enemy that is seducing Your creation to be a part of extremist groups, whose main purpose is to terrorize and mutilate Your sons and daughters. I declare the power of our Mighty God, El Gibbor, to be with us as we execute exploits against such groups (Isaiah 9:6, Strong# H1368). Satan, the Lord rebukes you (Zechariah 3:2)! May the church rise up in power, authority, confidence, and courage, proclaiming the gospel of Jesus Christ in this season. I denounce fear and doubt that the enemy tries to put in the hearts of God's people and throughout the earth. Father allow not one more victim to be harmed by the grips of Satan. I cancel every diabolical plot and scheme against Your children, who believes and proclaims salvation by none other than Christ Jesus. May the power that is in God's sons and daughters rise up unhindered in this generation and cause every extremist group to turn from their wicked ways, confess with their mouths that Jesus is their Savior, bow their knee and serve Christ Jesus (Romans 10:9). I declare that every weapon used by these extremist groups be put down and destroyed by the power of the only True and Living God, Elohim Chay (khah-e) (Jeremiah 10:10, Deuteronomy 5:26, Strong# H430, H2416). Your Word declares, "Have we not all one father? Hath not one God created us? Why do we deal treacherously every man against his brother, by profaning the covenant of our fathers" (Malachi 2:10)? Therefore, I decree and declare unity among Your people (Psalm 133:1-3). Now Lord may Your signs, wonders and healing power manifest to show forth the Glory of God in the earth and stop extremist groups in their diabolical tracks. For Your Word declares, "behold their threatenings: and grant unto thy servants, that with all boldness they may speak thy word, By stretching forth thine hand to heal; and that signs and wonders may be done by the name of thy holy child Jesus" (Acts 4:29-30). I command Your warring angels to take their positions and war against this demonic spirit and protect Your children (Psalm 91:10-13, Acts 12:7-11). I declare what has been an issue in the nations with extremist terrorist groups up to now, is no longer an issue. I declare there is not even a remnant or a memory of any extreme radical terrorist group. I declare the thought of another extreme group rising when one is eliminated, is canceled in Jesus name. I decree the hearts of every man, woman, boy and girl who have been seduced into violence, are now turned to God and the ways of the enemy have been dismantled from their lives. I decree their hearts now love all. I decree it to be so, by the power given to me, by the infallible Holy Word of God, in Jesus name, Amen.

My ears are open to hear your voice. Speak Lord!

_____

_____

Date Prayer Request Released   Date Prayer Answered

_____   _____

PRAYER AGAINST ANY WORSHIP OTHER THAN THE WORSHIP OF GOD THE CREATOR

Heavenly Father, I come against the use and worship of witchcraft, magic, sorcery, idols and gods that have been formed by the minds and hands of man. Abba Father, I declare Your children will make a vow and will adhere to our vow to love, honor, worship and serve You only, all the days of our lives. That releases us from any curse. I decree that we will not perish because we worship You Lord (Deuteronomy 8:19). I confess that You are our Lord. Jesus was sent as our Savior and there are no other gods that entice Your sons and daughters. I decree Your sons and daughters are free from the tricks of Satan to entice God's people into any form of idolatry. You Lord are our Creator and we serve You only because You are a jealous God (Exodus 34:14, Deuteronomy 6:15). I declare the world will not dictate to God's people who to serve. I declare that all creation of this world shall have a hunger and thirst to worship God, serve God and function in the mandates or the parameters of the Word of God. Lord, raise up fivefold ministers to teach Your people Your Word. Raise up Your children to take their mantles to preach, teach and prophecy to Your children to worship the only true and living God. I declare stumbling blocks shall be shattered at the name of the Most High God because we will only worship the Lord thy God (Ezekiel 14:4). Because we, Your children, have the DNA of God flowing through our veins we seek after the heart of God

(Genesis 1:27). We long for the presence of God, the Word of God and to worship the creator of our being. I declare that the Kingdom of God and the government of God shall arise if there be any earthly government that will declare a mandate to worship any other god. I declare that Your people will have the heart and boldness to proclaim who we will serve as the three Jewish boys (Daniel 3:1-30). Therefore, I declare that the sons and daughters of God speak out with authority against idol worship, witchcraft, magic, sorcery and satanic worship. The ways and decrees of God shall be declared and established in the earth realm today and thereafter. I declare that we were created to love You Lord, worship You Lord, honor You Lord, and that is what we shall do (Genesis 1:27, 1 Samuel 12:24). I decree it to be so, by the power given to me, by the infallible Holy Word of God, in Jesus name, Amen.

My ears are open to hear your voice. Speak Lord!

_____

_____

Date Prayer Request Released   Date Prayer Answered

_____   _____

102

PART V: PRAYERS FOR THE WORLD

PRAYER FOR CITY, STATE & NATION

Dear Heavenly Father, I pray for the salvation and peace for every city, state, country, and continents of the world. I declare that every gate to every city, state, country, continent and nation is open for the Glory of the Lord to enter in (Psalm 24:7). We welcome Your presence Lord in every corner of our world. Whatever has been holding countries back from loving You Lord is canceled and placed in the pits of hell. I decree every local, state and national leader is saved and filled with the Holy Spirit. I decree the earth is the Lord's including every neighborhood, community, city and state (Psalm 24:1). The sons and daughters of the Lord are great stewards of every resource on this earth. I decree our water systems are clean and free of disease and chemicals. I declare the chemical plants, petroleum refineries and all affiliated businesses that operate with potentially harmful substances in our communities, will have safe practices that do not pollute the air, ground or water supply surrounding its businesses. I declare the food industry will have a higher quality of breeding, farming, and handling of food sources. I declare foods are free of hormones, antibiotics, and fillers that are harmful to the human body. I declare every street in our communities will remain clean, free from violence and bringing Glory to God. I call for the freedom of every gang member in every community. I declare the Word of the Lord that God has given His sons and daughters cities and surrounding suburbs to dwell in, to be prosperous and give

Glory to God (Numbers 25:2). Your Word Lord declares, "the cities shall they have to dwell in; and the suburbs of them shall be for their cattle, and for their goods, and for all their beasts. And the suburbs of the cities, which ye shall give unto the Levites, shall reach from the wall of the city and outward a thousand cubits round about" (Numbers 35:3-4). Father, we thank You for this great gift of prosperous cities and suburbs. Lord, I command our cities shall be called cities of refuge (Numbers 35:11-15). Our communities are Holy and respected dwelling places for the Glory of God. I declare that our communities operate together in unity, love, mutual respect, encouraging each other and as we thrive as God designed us to thrive. Therefore, there will be no contention or strife in our homes, communities, cities, states, every border, and nation. We are the light of the world that shall never be hidden or fall prey to destruction (Matthew 5: 14-16). We give You Lord all the honor and glory for our peaceful and blessed cities, states and nations. I decree it to be so, by the power given to me, by the infallible Holy Word of God, in Jesus name, Amen.

My ears are open to hear your voice. Speak Lord!

_____

_____

Date Prayer Request Released   Date Prayer Answered

_____   _____

PRAYER FOR DEVELOPING COUNTRIES

Dear Heavenly Father, I cry out for Your people in developing countries. I decree and declare that developing countries will no longer be called by that name. Father, You created "heaven and the earth" and You said it is good (Genesis 1:1, 31). Therefore, I speak that the corruption of these countries will cease now so that their country is no longer developing but already developed. I declare that every country, nation, city, state, province, and land is established at the Word of God. Father although you said, "the poor will be with us always", Jesus said, if I have visited the sick, hungry, thirsty, naked and clothed those in need and visited those in jail I have done the same for Jesus (Matthew 25:35-46). So I declare that the poverty level is diminished and finally demolished in every nation, to every corner of the earth. I decree that Your people Lord are fed, clothed and have every need met. Father, I decree that You have given Your sons and daughters a heart to love and give abundantly as You Lord are a giver, and have given to Your children. When Your sons and daughters see Your people in need, we see You and are able to give our services to Your people. Father raise up people that have the ability to develop services, build homes, businesses and organizations for those who are in need. I decree every nation is flourishing and its people flourish. No nation is in debt. No nation is poor and no nation is destitute. I decree that all those in governmental or decision-making positions are free from corruption.

Father, I pray for Godly leaders that will speak and stand for Your people in these flourishing nations. Shatter the chains of poverty that restrict Your sons and daughters from having and living a life of abundance and destiny. I decree that women and children are no longer devalued but respected and honored as God has destined. Favor surrounds God's sons and daughters and every developing country. I decree and declare clean water, clean living areas, and disease free nations. I decree Your Word, "And I will sow them among the people: and they shall remember me in far countries; and they shall live with their children, and turn again. And I will strengthen them in the Lord; and they shall walk up and down in his name, saith the Lord" (Zechariah 10:9, 12). The favor of the Lord rests upon every nation and thereby every need is met in every nation. Those that are wealthy see our brothers and sisters and never turn our backs against God's sons and daughters, but lends to those who need assistance. For Your Word declares,

If there be among you a poor man of one of thy brethren within any of thy gates in thy land which the Lord thy God giveth thee, thou shalt not harden thine heart, nor shut thine hand from thy poor brother: But thou shalt open thine hand wide unto him, and shalt surely lend him sufficient for his need, in that which he wanteth. Beware that there be not a thought in thy wicked heart, saying, The seventh year, the year of release, is at hand; and thine eye be evil against thy poor brother, and thou givest him nought;

and he cry unto the Lord against thee, and it be sin unto thee. Thou shalt surely give him, and thine heart shall not be grieved when thou givest unto him: because that for this thing the Lord thy God shall bless thee in all thy works, and in all that thou puttest thine hand unto. For the poor shall never cease out of the land: therefore I command thee, saying, Thou shalt open thine hand wide unto thy brother, to thy poor, and to thy needy, in thy land **(Deuteronomy 15:7-11).**

Therefore, just as the Father withholds no good thing from His sons and daughters, we will function as a representative of our Father and give out of our abundance, as He has given freely to us (Psalm 84:11). I decree it to be so, by the power given to me, by the infallible Holy Word of God, in Jesus name, Amen.

My ears are open to hear your voice. Speak Lord!

_____

_____

Date Prayer Request Released   Date Prayer Answered

_____   _____

PRAYER FOR SCHOOLS, CHURCHES, HOSPITALS, CLINICS AND RECREATION IN DEVELOPING COUNTRIES

Heavenly Father, I decree that I have the wisdom of God to count up the cost for every business deal, every building, every development and every person assigned to build and be employed in these developments (Luke 14:28). Your Word says, "Except the Lord build the house, they labour in vain that build it: except the Lord keep the city, the watchman waketh but in vain" (Psalm 127:1). Therefore, Father God lead every project, every building and all assignments for these projects. I command my ears to be open to hearing Your will, Your design and Your plans for every detail. Just as You gave Moses the exact dimensions of the tabernacle I ask that You will download every dimension and detail for every project that You give. I confess that You Lord will even make every provision available for these projects. Father anoint and ordain the pastors, elders and ministry leaders for every church planted. May they all have the heart of God and for God as David. Anoint all of the administrators, teachers and volunteers for every school planted. Download the appropriate curriculums for every planted school in every nation. Provide the necessary equipment needed for the schools. Anoint all hospital/clinic administrators, nurses, doctors, technicians, caregivers, and provide all necessary equipment. Because I commit to You Lord in all that I do, You Lord establish the plans down to the minute detail of every project that builds lasting resources for Your people (Proverbs 16:3). I declare that every need is met "according to his riches in glory by Christ Jesus" (Philippians 4:19). Father, I pray that Your sons and daughters who have been starved of education for any reason be nourished now. Whatever obstacles that have been holding Your precious creation back from being educated and well informed is broken now. For Your Word declares, "My people are destroyed for lack of knowledge: because thou hast rejected knowledge, I will also reject thee, that thou shalt be no priest to me: seeing thou hast forgotten the law of thy God, I will also forget thy children" (Hosea 4:6). I decree Your sons and daughters are no longer in the position to perish because we have every opportunity to learn; we have the right tools and we run to every institution for learning. Your people Lord fill the house of the Lord to learn more of You and to receive divine revelation for strategic moves and direction. I decree Your wisdom and knowledge saturate every community, city, state, providence and country including rural areas. I declare every nation is flourishing because God has allowed a new atmosphere to manifest in every planted church, school, hospital clinic and business which is all for the Glory of God. Father connect divine relationships, business partnerships and political connections that will accelerate the plans of God among every nation. I decree it to be so, by the power given to me, by the infallible Holy Word of God, in Jesus name, Amen.

My ears are open to hear your voice. Speak Lord!

_____

_____

Date Prayer Request Released   Date Prayer Answered

_____   _____

PRAYER FOR OUR GOVERNMEMT OFFICIALS

Heavenly Father I seek You for the selection and maintenance of those in positions who make decisions for a large group of people. For Your Word declares, "supplications, prayers, intercessions, and giving of thanks, be made for all men; For kings, and for all that are in authority; that we may lead a quiet and peaceable life in all godliness and honesty" (1Timothy 2:1-2). We seek You because we know that You hold all power and wisdom in Your hands. Heavenly Father, I lift up prayers now for those in leadership roles in every government system in the United States and in every nation in the world. For this is good and acceptable in the sight of God our Saviour;" (1 Timothy 2:3). Therefore, if it is acceptable and good to our Heavenly Father, we count it as wisdom and will adhere to Your Word. I decree and declare we will have leaders in government that love God, have the heart of God and leads according to the words given by God. I decree all leaders in all governments will have a heart and love the people. May all the leaders of the government of the United States and the governments in all nations be in unity, for we know that there is anointing in unity (Psalm 133:1-3). Therefore, I declare that all governments are speaking the same God filled information, on one accord with the same mindset, which is the mind of Christ (Romans 15:5-6, 1 Peter 3:8). Because the governments are in one accord, there is nothing that each government cannot do. For Lord, we know Your Word declares, "if a house be divided against itself, that house cannot stand (Mark 3:25). I decree that every need is met in every state, country, and nation. Our country is flourishing because we have great Godly counsel (Proverbs 29:2). I thank You for the multitude of counsel for I decree that Your people and the land You gave us will prosper (Proverbs 11:14). It is the Lord's will that all nations prosper, as we seek the will of the Father and follow His commands (Jeremiah 29:7, 1 Timothy 2:4). Abba Father, as this is the year of elections for the United States President, I decree that the right Godly person is chosen to fill that position. Speak to the presidential candidate and give them Your wisdom, knowledge, and understanding. Give them direction on what to do and what to say, not only in this election to gain trust of the American people to win, but also to give the Presidential candidate what to say after the election when leading Your people in the United States. May the presidential candidate represent humility, integrity and the Spirit of God. Holiness is the stance that the presidential candidate operates in. I decree it to be so, by the power given to me, by the infallible Holy Word of God, in Jesus name, Amen.

My ears are open to hear your voice. Speak Lord!

_____

_____

Date Prayer Request Released   Date Prayer Answered

_____   _____

116

PRAYER FOR MISSIONARIES

Dear Heavenly Father, You said, "The harvest truly is plenteous, but the labourers are few; Pray ye therefore the Lord of the harvest, that he will send forth labourers into his harvest" (Mathew 9: 37-38). I pray for laborers to come forth to work to gather the harvest. Because You Father are Jehovah Jireh the Lord who provides, You provide for every laborer in the field. When You Lord called the disciples and told them to follow, You also provided for them (Mathew 4:19-20). Jesus You said, "go thou to the sea, and cast an hook, and take up the fish that first cometh up; and when thou hast opened his mouth, thou shalt find a piece of money: that take, and give unto them for me and thee" (Mathew 17:27). Hallelujah! Therefore, Father give us the exact location of which the following are located for us; possessions, finances, provisions and whatever is required of us when we enter any nation. Give us the strategy to get these provisions down to the very detail. Just as You provided for the disciples, You provide for us. I declare the provision of residence, food, clothing, travel guides, local native tongue interpreters, local military or security officials, transportation, supplies for the territory, and willing participants for every project. I pray Lord that You assign prayer warriors to be positioned on the wall praying constantly for those on the mission field (Colossians 4:2-3). Their prayer is strategic in praying for open doors, provisions, boldness, the spread of the gospel, protection, guidance, wisdom, and regeneration of those on assignment on the field (Colossians 1: 11,19, 4:2-3; Ephesians 6:19; 2 Thessalonians 3:1-2; Romans 15:30; 2 Corinthians 1:11). Help your servants to have a heart of God that overflows to every region that they are assigned. I pray that every physical and emotional need is met. Each missionary has the joy, peace, and rest of the Lord. I pray that missionaries that carry the gospel of Jesus are protected from jail, threats, and attacks of the enemy. I pray that every leader in the field has the same confidence and power to rebuke Satan and his evil attacks by speaking authority and casting the enemy out from the people and that region (Acts 16:16-18). I decree that a blazing hedge of protection and the blood of Jesus surround missionaries which make them untouchable by any unclean spirit or weapon set for them. I decree and declare the apostolic anointing over every missionary. I pray that they are poured into by apostles, prophets, pastors, evangelists and teachers so that they can pour out to every region in which they are called. I pray that You will send them an apostolic team so they can flow through the regions blazing trails through power, authority, with signs, wonders, miracles and healing (1 Corinthians 12:28). I decree it to be so, by the power given to me, by the infallible Holy Word of God, in Jesus name, Amen.

My ears are open to hear your voice. Speak Lord!

_____

_____

Date Prayer Request Released   Date Prayer Answered

_____   _____

PRAYERS FOR THE STATE OF THE WORLD

Heavenly Father we pray for the peace of God to manifest in the world. Darkness will not invade Your world (Luke 1:79). I declare that every inkling of confusion is cast to the pits of hell for God is not the author of confusion (1 Corinthians 14:33). I declare the freedom of every human in every nation. I declare the chains that are hindering countries from growth, prosperity and serving God are broken off now! I declare the salvation of every nation. I declare every nation believes, serves and calls on the name of Jesus. We are free as Your Word declares, "If the Son therefore shall make you free, ye shall be free indeed" (John 8:36). May the nations arise and awaken to the commands of God (Numbers 23:24, Joel 3:12). Shake and arouse the nations to fulfill Your purpose and destiny in the earth that the desires of all nations will manifest and the true unhindered Glory of God be revealed (Haggai 2:7). May the earth be saturated with the wisdom, knowledge, understanding and the fullness of the Glory of God (Habakkuk 2:14). I declare that worship goes forth to the only true and living God, Elohim Chay (khah-e) (the living God), that God's anger is not kindled to the destruction of nations (Jeremiah 10:10, Strong# H430, H2416). Assemble your nations together to be in full operation that Your mighty works can take place (Isaiah 43:9). Because we are in one accord with the Spirit of God, I decree there is no communication breakdown among God's nations. Your nations accomplish everything that You set it to accomplish and that is to serve You. Your Word declares, "the kingdom is the Lord's: and he is the governor among the nations" (Psalm 22:28). Therefore, govern all nations that there is no one lacking any good thing (Psalm 84:11). I declare that the economy of every nation is flourishing that poverty no longer exists. Every person that has been chosen to lead a nation loves and serves God and therefore denounces corruptive behaviors. I rebuke Satan. The Lord rebukes you and your plots and schemes to keep the nation in conflict and desiring war (Zechariah 3:2). I decree Your Word Lord, "When a man's ways please the Lord, he maketh even his enemies to be at peace with him" (Proverbs 16:7). Therefore, conflict is demolished at the hand of God that causes peace to go forth among all nations. I decree it to be so, by the power given to me, by the infallible Holy Word of God, in Jesus name, Amen.

My ears are open to hear your voice. Speak Lord!

_____

_____

Date Prayer Request Released   Date Prayer Answered

_____   _____

122

PART VI: PRAYERS FOR ECONOMIC GROWTH & DEVELOPMENT

PRAYER FOR ECONOMIC EMPOWERMENT

Dear Heavenly Father, I decree supernatural transfers are happening now in the spirit realm. Because Your sons and daughters seek You, we shall lack no good thing of the Lord (Psalms 34:10). Our nations are blessed because we serve You, Lord. I decree Your Word, "Blessed is the nation whose God is the Lord; and the people whom he hath chosen for his own inheritance" (Psalms 33:12). Therefore, I decree that the stock market does not determine the wealth of our nation but is only a minuscule scale of the wealth of our nations that comes from only the Most High God. I decree our nations are flowing with wealth, riches, and resources beyond measure because we are obedient to the Word of God (Exodus 33:3). Because Your sons and daughters are obedient to Your Word, we humble ourselves and seek Your face daily, therefore You have healed our land (2 Chronicles 7:14). Your Word declares, "If ye be willing and obedient, ye shall eat the good of the land" (Isaiah 1:19). Therefore, I declare the obedience of every nation that we may dwell in peace and enjoy the fruits of the land. I declare that Your sons and daughters are owners of property, land, businesses, enterprises and corporations and therefore, the economy is strong, buoyant and continuously flourishing. Therefore, the employment rate is beyond what could ever be imagined. I decree there is no break in prosperity in any nations' economy, but a continuous overflow of abundance. I decree there is no famine, lack or poverty in any nation because

Your sons and daughters take care of our brothers and sisters (Proverbs 19:17, Matthew 25:35-40). I decree the worship of God the Father in every nation. I decree every nation shall glorify the true and living God with our lips, our life and all resources given to us. I decree and declare Your people are great stewards of the land and resources that have been given unto us (Matthew 25: 14-23). Therefore, You provide Your sons and daughters with even more resources, wealth and riches all for the Glory and Kingdom of God. I decree it to be so, by the power given to me, by the infallible Holy Word of God, in Jesus name, Amen.

My ears are open to hear your voice. Speak Lord!

_____

_____

Date Prayer Request Released   Date Prayer Answered

_____   _____

PRAYER FOR TERRITORY

Dear Heavenly Father, I ask that You would give me new territory. For Your Word says, "the earth is the Lords and the fullness thereof" (Psalm 24:1). Therefore, because I am Your child I ask that You would release unchartered territory to me now. This territory will be used to build for Your people, to have a people to serve You, to praise and worship You. Therefore, I decree Your Word because I love you Lord and walk in obedience to Your Holy Word; You will bless me in the land and cause me to take possession of the unchartered land that I enter (Deuteronomy 30:16). Father, "enlarge thy coast" and give me unchartered territory (Deuteronomy 19:8, 1 Chronicles 4:10). Father, I decree that the place that we have been in is bursting at the seams and can no longer hold me, my family and my gift. Therefore, I pray that my dwelling and place of influence be enlarged, stretched, lengthened and strengthened for my family and me (Isaiah 54:2). I acknowledge You Lord for only You are able to extend the borders of my territory (Isaiah 26:15). Father, You promised land to Abraham, the Israelites and others in the Bible. Because You, Lord, are not a respecter of persons I pray You grant land unto me (Genesis 17:8, Acts10:34, Romans 2:11). Father, show Your sons and daughters the land that is for us and give the necessary provisions to allow us to take possession of the land. Lord, You said, "Ask of me, and I shall give thee the heathen for thine inheritance, and the uttermost parts of the earth for thy possession"

(Psalm 2:8). Therefore, we ask for our inheritance and the uttermost parts of the earth, not selfishly for ourselves but to expand the Kingdom of God for Your sons and daughters. Because we are joint heirs with Christ, we have the ability to own what our Father in Heaven releases to us (Romans 8:17). Therefore, we pray that land, acreage, homes, apartment complexes, duplexes, business districts and stores in our community, surrounding areas and in every nation are released and belong to Your children who are obedient to Your Word. You said, "A good man leaveth an inheritance to his children's children: and the wealth of the sinner is laid up for the just" (Proverbs 13:22). Therefore, I declare that our inheritance is here and our wealth is in our hands now. Father Your Word declares that the inheritance of our Father can be transferred to His children (Numbers 27:4-11). Therefore, we call forth all land and properties from our forefathers, all those in my blood line and the possession of my Heavenly Father to be transferred to us now. Lord remove the blinders from our eyes that we may see the land that You have prepared for us (Numbers 27:12). Lord, "Enlarge the place of thy tent, and let them stretch forth the curtains of thine habitations: spare not, lengthen thy cords, and strengthen thy stakes; For thou shalt break forth on the right hand and on the left; and thy seed shall inherit the Gentiles, and make the desolate cities to be inhabited" (Isaiah 54:2-3). Thank You, Lord, that You cause me to possess every uncharted land and even land of the wicked is being released unto me because I honor Your name, love You and adhere to Your Word (Deuteronomy 30:16). For

Lord You commanded, "this day to love the Lord thy God, to walk in his ways, and to keep his commandments and his statutes and his judgments, that thou mayest live and multiply: and the Lord thy God shall bless thee in the land whither thou goest to possess it" (Deuteronomy 30:16). I decree and declare your Holy Word that You go before Your people to make a way and get our land ready for us (Isaiah 45:2-3) I decree it to be so, by the power given to me, by the infallible Holy Word of God, in Jesus name, Amen.

My ears are open to hear your voice. Speak Lord!

_____

_____

Date Prayer Request Released   Date Prayer Answered

_____   _____

PRAYER FOR OWNERSHIP
(WE ARE NOT RENTERS)

Dear Heavenly Father thank You for the ability to own. We are owners and developers and not renters. Our headquarters in Heaven says that we serve a God that has a kingdom government that mandates that we are heirs to the Kingdom of God and therefore have supernatural access to finances, riches and witty inventions to build with no lingering expenses. I pray that we are debt free. Therefore, we hold no mortgages. We do not sign for mortgages because we have all the necessary resources to pay off every home, business, and building that we decide to purchase. I declare, "The earth is the Lord's, and the fullness thereof; the world, and they that dwell therein" (Psalm 24:1). Therefore, the sons and daughters of God have a right to His possessions because we serve God. Father, You said, "The heaven, even the heavens, are the Lord's: but the earth hath he given to the children of men" (Psalm 115:16). Therefore, we have no business renting what already has been given to us. We are owners and not renters. Father God I declare that Your children will remember for the rest of our days that it is You that gives us the ability to get wealth, maintain it and the ability to own and not rent (Deuteronomy 8:18). Father, we have received the revelation that renting holds Your people indebted to others and therefore I confess, that Your people are free from the mindset of renting, we possess the kingship mentality of owning land, property, and businesses. Because

Your sons and daughters seek and serve You, Lord, we shall receive the blessings of the Lord (Psalms 24:5-6). Thank You Lord that You promised land to Abraham and his descendants and because of Your Son Jesus we may now take part in ownership of land that You have given for us to govern as stewards until Christ returns (Gen. 12:7; 13:15; 15:18; 26:4; Ex. 32:13). I decree that as You told Abram to lift up his head, Your sons and daughters lift up our heads and look to the north south east and west and tread our feet on the land that has been given to us (Genesis 13:14, 16-17). Because You have given Your sons and daughters favor to have and own land, I declare altars will be built all over the world to give honor to You Lord (Genesis 13:18). Lord Your Word declares the giving of countries as an inheritance to Your sons and daughters (Genesis 26:4). This is our inheritance for years to come (Exodus 32:13). Lord, I decree and declare that Your children are holding fast to Your Word and "wholly follow your word" and receive Your promise as Caleb did (Deuteronomy 1:36). I decree it to be so, by the power given to me, by the infallible Holy Word of God, in Jesus name, Amen.

My ears are open to hear your voice. Speak Lord!

_____

_____

Date Prayer Request Released   Date Prayer Answered

_____   _____

PRAYER FOR SUPERNATURAL DEBT CANCELATION

Father God You said in Your Word that the children of God are lenders and not borrowers. No man and no company will hold Your people captive by a bill or outrageous interest rates to keep Your sons and daughters paying for multiple years. I decree that our mortgages, credit card bills, car notes, student loans and other loans are paid off in full and we owe nothing to man. Just as Your Word God declares jubilee every fifty years, I declare that Your people experience jubilee now. All debts are forgiven. I call out for the **"LORD'S RELEASE"** now (Deuteronomy 15:2)! I declare Your Word, "At the end of every seven years thou shalt make a release. And this is the manner of the release: Every creditor that lendeth ought unto his neighbour shall release it; he shall not exact it of his neighbour, or of his brother; because it is called the **"LORD'S RELEASE"** (Deuteronomy 15:1-2). Therefore, we are released from all debts now! It is not Your desire for Your children to be in debt because it keeps us from fulfilling our destiny. Because we are heirs to the throne of God through Jesus Christ, what the Father has, is what we have. Your sons and daughters have dominion and power on earth (Genesis 1:27-28). We are a royal priesthood (1 Peter 2:9). We are God's Kingdom ambassadors. Therefore, we represent the Kingdom of God and nothing is withheld from Your children. We have the favor of God. We are great stewards of all the financial resources entrusted to us. We will not bury our resources as Jesus said a man did in a parable (Matthew 25:14-18). Our God has blessed us as he has promised and therefore, we will lend to many nations, but we will not borrow; and we will rule over many nations, but they will not rule over us (Deuteronomy 15:6). I confess that it is well with Your sons and daughters because we are gracious and lend and therefore our cause is maintained in judgment (Psalm 9:4, 112:5). When we make a vow, we honor and complete our vow with no hesitation (Ecclesiastes 5:4). Therefore, our name is great in the land (Proverbs 22:1). Your sons and daughters have the wisdom of God and make wise decisions as good stewards of all resources entrusted by God to us. I decree that the spirit of poverty is off our lives and all of our familial blood line. I decree it to be so, by the power given to me, by the infallible Holy Word of God, in Jesus name, Amen.

My ears are open to hear your voice. Speak Lord!

_____

_____

Date Prayer Request Released   Date Prayer Answered

_____   _____

PRAYER FOR TRANSPORTATION

Dear Heavenly Father, I thank You for the ability to own transportation. I decree that Your sons and daughters have reliable transportation that does not affect the community in which we live. I declare that we shall not drive dilapidated cars, trucks or any other form of transportation. I declare that we as Your sons and daughters, are great stewards of every form of transportation that You have given to us. As we look for the purchase of new transportation, I declare that we already have favor among all dealers. Therefore, we get the best deals for the best form of transportation. I decree because we are children of the Most High God, we drive the best and operate in excellence. Father, those who rely on public transportation, I declare every public alternate transportation system is professional, elegant and meets the Kingdom of God standards. I declare public transportation will be kept clean and is reasonably priced, that it will be desirable to all. I decree multiple careers will be established for excellent public transportation. I cancel every attack from the enemy for accidents, derailments, explosions and terror attacks. I command the Word of God, "And the Lord said unto Satan, The Lord rebuke thee, O Satan; even the Lord that hath chosen Jerusalem rebuke thee: is not this a brand plucked out of the fire" (Zechariah 3:2)? Now, Lord we ask for excellent built aircrafts and technology of tracking aircrafts. I decree and declare that You Lord are raising up men and women with the wisdom of the Lord to create a crash resistant aircraft with capabilities to save passengers in emergency situations. I decree that the plans of the Lord for improved aircrafts will be approved and in operation in this year because of the accelerated favor of the Lord. I decree and declare the cruise ships will be operating at all times in excellence. There will be no more accidents or incidents while in use. Even cruise ships that transport Your sons and daughters for the purpose of relaxation will be built, maintained in excellence and operated by the best. I decree there will be no more deplorable living situations upon these ships. May these cruise lines always have the best ships, clean and operating at full capacity. I declare these ships are built to last and therefore will not breakdown nor be stranded in the middle of oceans. I decree it to be so, by the power given to me, by the infallible Holy Word of God, in Jesus name, Amen.

My ears are open to hear your voice. Speak Lord!

_____

_____

Date Prayer Request Released   Date Prayer Answered

_____   _____

PRAYER FOR FINANCES
(WEALTH CREATION)

Heavenly Father, I pray that Your sons and daughters are wealthy and have more than enough to accomplish what You have called us to do. Because You Lord have given us wealth, we help the poor and give with a grateful heart unto You Lord. It is You, Lord, that "maketh" Your children "rich and adds no sorrow" (Proverbs 10:22). I declare that the wealth of the wicked that has been laid up for Your heirs is released unto us now (Proverbs 13:22). I declare because Your children are faithful tithers and not robbers of God, You have opened up the windows of Heaven and poured out blessings that we don't even have room enough to receive (Malachi 3:8). I declare Your children plan ahead to give unto the Kingdom by putting aside and saving what belongs to God (1 Corinthians 16:2). Your sons and daughters understand that wealth is not just for us, but for the Kingdom of God. So we release some of our wealth to the Kingdom helping the poor, helping the widows, helping the nations, helping our city, state and community. Because Your sons and daughters are wealthy, those around us receive the same overflow that we possess. Nothing or no one around Your people is poor or dilapidated. We are able to "leave an inheritance" to our "children's children" (Proverb 13:22). Because we give to others it shall be given to us with, "good measure, pressed down, and shaken together and running over. For with the same measure that ye mete withal it shall be measured to you again" (Luke 6:38). Overflow is pouring into our lives. Because we reverence and delight in Jehovah Jireh's commandments, wealth and riches are in our home (Psalm 112:1-3). The curse of poverty is reversed. I declare Your Word that Your sons and daughters are heirs to the throne (Romans 8:17). We carry the promise. We have been made kings and priests and have been given power and authority to reign on earth by the blood of the Lamb (Revelation 5:10). Your Word declares, "That I may cause those that love me to inherit substance; and I will fill their treasures" (Proverbs 8:21). Therefore, because we love You we have an inheritance and treasures. I decree it to be so, by the power given to me, by the infallible Holy Word of God, in Jesus name, Amen.

My ears are open to hear your voice. Speak Lord!

_____

_____

Date Prayer Request Released   Date Prayer Answered

_____   _____

PRAYER FOR BUSINESSES (DEVELOPMENT, MAINTENANCE & FUTURE SUCCESS)

Heavenly Father, I decree that all of Your children have entrepreneurial spirits and own businesses. Because God created us in his image and likeness, we have the Spirit of God and are creators and leaders. God You said, "Let us make **MAN** in **OUR IMAGE**, after our **LIKENESS**: and let them have **DOMINION** over the fish of the sea, and over the fowl of the air, and over the cattle, and **OVER ALL THE EARTH**, and over every creeping thing that creepeth upon the earth" (Genesis 1:26). Because we were born in Your image and made to have dominion, we are innovators. We have the same Spirit to create. We wait for no one to start a business idea first, we just start. We are therefore leaders in our communities, cities, states, regions and nations. We **BLAZE THE TRAILS** in creating and maintaining top of the line businesses, enterprises, and corporations. I declare my vision is clear, written and plain so that others see and run with the vision given by God to me (Habakkuk 2:2). I decree and declare that You Lord give the resources for the development, to maintain every business, enterprise, and corporation and allow it to thrive. I thank You, Lord that every Christian owned business, enterprise, and corporation increases the property value in the community in which it resides. Every business, enterprise and corporation run by Your people excels and thrives in the community. The community is the better because every business, enterprise, and corporation run by Your children are professional, have the Spirit of God and is in operation with integrity. I decree and declare that God's people are employed at every excellent business, enterprise, and corporation. These Godly employees are sent by the Most High God and make the best team, like no other. Every team member is a child of God, creative, witty, intelligent and extraordinarily excellent in their craft. Every team member fills in the gap that may be lacking. They are the essential link in the chain that makes our company extraordinarily strong, prosperous and successful. They bring even more to the business than our business can ever ask or imagine (Ephesians 3:20). Christian business, enterprise, and corporation owners are plentiful and have extraordinary amounts of clientele and resources. There is an extraordinary overflow of jobs, careers, and franchises created from our businesses, enterprises, and corporations. Every Christian business, enterprise, and corporation owner is a leader in the community in which they reside. They build the community with resources given back to the community in which they reside. I decree that Christian business, enterprise, and corporation owners are operating under the apostolic anointing. I say that all believers of the gospel of Jesus Christ have creative minds to build, create products and start a business, enterprise, and corporation. I decree that we all are leaders and will take the steps necessary to begin and complete every project leading to the start of a business, enterprise and corporation and its operation. We all complete every project that we start because we have a finishers' heart. I declare we are, "confident of this very thing, that he which hath begun a good work in [us] will perform it until the day of Jesus Christ:" (Philippians 1:6). Therefore, we will "Commit thy works unto the Lord, and thy thoughts shall be established" (Proverbs 16:3). I declare Your Word Lord, "whatsoever [we] do, [we] do it heartily, as to the Lord, and not unto men; Knowing that of the Lord [we] shall receive the reward of the inheritance: for [we] serve the Lord Christ" (Colossians 3:23-24). I declare that we have laser sharp focus on every project leading to the beginning and success of our business, enterprise, and corporation. I decree that God inspires every creative thought, gives the motivation to thrive and gives guidance in our business, enterprise, and corporation. Father God, download every detail of the building process, our market, advertising, maintenance, hiring, training and maintaining employees, insurance, how to excel in profit margin and every detail necessary to run a successful business. We walk the perimeter of every business, enterprise, and corporation praying over the foundation, consecrating and dedicating the building, plans and ideas to You Lord. Every assignment of the enemy to frustrate Gods' purpose and His plan is canceled and cut off at the root. Even as our business becomes extraordinarily successful, we will always pause and give thanks to You Lord. Time will be set aside to praise, worship and honor you Lord. Time will also be set aside for vacation and spending quality dedicated time with our spouse and family. We always keep in the forefront of our minds: it's all about

You! The success of a business, enterprise and corporation are to draw people to You and to support the Kingdom. It is not just for Your people to get wealthy and forget about others. Therefore, we seek you daily to prioritize and get revelation on where our wealth will be utilized in the Kingdom of God. I decree it to be so, by the power given to me, by the infallible Holy Word of God, in Jesus name, Amen.

My ears are open to hear your voice. Speak Lord!

_____

_____

Date Prayer Request Released   Date Prayer Answered

_____   _____

About the Author

Apostle Sonya Hurst accepted Jesus Christ at a young age and received the Holy Spirit at age 23. She immediately started exercising her spiritual gifts within the body of Christ. This included teaching Sunday school, ministering at nursing homes, serving the community through feeding the homeless, missions abroad and maintaining an active prayer life. She is married to Apostle Jonathan Hurst and they have two daughters. Sonya has degrees in biology and nursing. Her nursing profession allows her to minister to the medical and spiritual needs of many. She serves as a prayer partner at Lakewood Church. She was recently ordained an Apostle by International Covenant Life Network. Her long-term goals are: to help those in developing countries see the manifestation of their full potential in God; design curriculums, plant schools, churches, hospitals, clinics, and restore and build communities.

www.sonyahurstministries.com

CPSIA information can be obtained
at www.ICGtesting.com
Printed in the USA
LVHW080257180223
739780LV00033B/1044

9 781945 456350